NATIONAL DEFENSE RESEARCH INSTITUTE

data_flood

Helping the Navy Address the Rising Tide of Sensor Information

Isaac R. Porche III • Bradley Wilson

Erin-Elizabeth Johnson

Shane Tierney • Evan Saltzman

Prepared for the Office of the United States Navy

Approved for public release; distribution unlimited

This research was sponsored by the Department of the Navy and conducted within the Acquisition and Technology Policy Center of the RAND National Defense Research Institute, a federally funded research and development center sponsored by the Office of the Secretary of Defense, the Joint Staff, the Unified Combatant Commands, the Navy, the Marine Corps, the defense agencies, and the defense Intelligence Community.

Library of Congress Control Number: 2014938348

ISBN: 978-0-8330-8429-3

The RAND Corporation is a nonprofit institution that helps improve policy and decisionmaking through research and analysis. RAND's publications do not necessarily reflect the opinions of its research clients and sponsors.

Support RAND—make a tax-deductible charitable contribution at www.rand.org/giving/contribute.html

RAND® is a registered trademark

Cover by Pete Soriano

© Copyright 2014 RAND Corporation

RAND OFFICES

SANTA MONICA, CA • WASHINGTON, DC

PITTSBURGH, PA • NEW ORLEANS, LA • JACKSON, MS • BOSTON, MA

CAMBRIDGE, UK • BRUSSELS, BE

www.rand.org

Preface

The title of this report was inspired by the comments of former U.S. Air Force intelligence lead Lt Gen David A. Deptula (ret.), who forecast in 2012 that his service would soon be "swimming in sensors and drowning in data" from unmanned air vehicles.[1] This report provides a summary of results from two studies conducted by the RAND Corporation for the U.S. Navy. The overarching concern in both studies was the "flood" of data coming from the intelligence, surveillance, and reconnaissance (ISR) systems that Navy intelligence analysts and commanders rely on for situational awareness. The first study identified the year in which the effects of this "flood" would first be felt (2016).[2] The second constituted the analysis of alternatives for the Distributed Common Ground System–Navy Increment 2, a system intended to help the Navy address the influx of data. This report describes the Navy's "big data" challenge and outlines potential solutions involving changes along four dimensions: people, tools and technology, data and data architecture, and demand and demand management. We also discuss broader issues related to the challenges and opportunities pre-

---

[1] Stew Magnuson, "Military 'Swimming in Sensors and Drowning in Data,'" *National Defense Magazine*, January 2010.

[2] Ed Brady, Jim Bexfield, Jim Hildegrand, and John Orem, "Analytical Approaches to Airborne ISR MORS Workshop: A Summary of Results from the Perspective of the Synthesis and Integration Group," presentation at the National Defense University, Washington, D.C., June 25, 2012; Isaac R. Porche III, Bradley Wilson, Shane Tierney, Ray Koym, James Dryden, Evan Saltzman, Roland J. Yardley, John M. Yurchak, Stephanie Young, Endy M. Daehner, Megan McKernan, and Kate Giglio, *The DCGS-Navy Increment 2 Analysis of Alternatives: Options for Meeting the TCPED Challenges and Opportunities*, Santa Monica, Calif.: RAND Corporation, 2013.

sented by ISR data. This report should be of interest to the Navy and other services, agencies, and organizations that rely on ISR data.

This report is, in essence, an executive summary of several longer, more-detailed reports, including a peer-reviewed briefing presented at a Military Operations Research Society Airborne ISR workshop.[3]

This research was sponsored by the Department of the Navy and conducted within the Acquisition and Technology Policy Center of the RAND National Defense Research Institute, a federally funded research and development center sponsored by the Office of the Secretary of Defense, the Joint Staff, the Unified Combatant Commands, the Navy, the Marine Corps, the defense agencies, and the defense Intelligence Community. Questions and comments about this research are welcome and should be directed to the project leader, Isaac Porche, at Isaac_Porche@rand.org, or to the center director, Cynthia Cook (Cynthia_Cook@rand.org)

For more information on the RAND Acquisition and Technology Policy Center, see http://www.rand.org/nsrd/ndri/centers/atp

---

[3]   A summary of proceedings for the entire workshop is at Brady et al., 2012.

Contents

Figures

Tables

Summary

U.S. Navy intelligence, surveillance, and reconnaissance (ISR) functions have become critical to U.S. national security over the last two decades.[1] Within the Navy, there is a growing demand for ISR data from drones and other sources that provide situational awareness, which helps Navy vessels avoid collisions, pinpoint targets, and perform a host of other mission-critical tasks.

The amount of data generated by ISR systems has, however, become overwhelming. All of the data collected by the Navy—and available from other sources, both government and commercial—are potentially useful, but processing them and deriving useful knowledge from them are severely taxing the analytical capabilities of the Navy's humans and networks. As the Navy acquires and fields new and additional sensors for collecting data, this "big data" challenge will continue to grow. Indeed, if the Navy continues to field sensors as planned but does not change the way it processes, exploits, and disseminates information, it will reach an ISR "tipping point"—the point at which intelligence analysts are no longer able to complete a minimum number of exploitation tasks within given time constraints—as soon as 2016.[2]

Today, as little as 5 percent of the data collected by ISR platforms actually reach the Navy analysts who need to see them. In the case of

---

[1] The Joint Chiefs of Staff defines ISR as the "synchronized, integrated planning and operation of sensors, processing, exploitation and dissemination systems in direct support of current and future operations." It also states that this is "an integrated intelligence and operations function" (Joint Chiefs of Staff, *Department of Defense Dictionary of Military and Associated Terms*, November 8, 2010, as amended through July 15, 2012).

[2] Brady et al., 2012; Porche et al., 2013.

analysts working afloat on ships, a large part of the problem is attributable to extremely slow download times caused by bandwidth and connectivity limitations. Analysts face other challenges to the timely consumption of data, including having to share access to communications pipelines with other organizations and having to download multiple pieces of large data (such as high-resolution images) to find exactly what they need. Most of the time, analysts do not have the luxury of receiving the "right" data in a timely fashion.

Today's analysts also face a wide variety of data streaming in from different platforms and sensors—data they must integrate (or fuse) to ensure accurate, comprehensive situational awareness. Their workstations are cluttered with different software applications and monitors that rely on data that often reside in separate databases or on separate networks. These factors degrade analysts' ability to integrate and fuse multiple intelligence types accurately, quickly, and thoroughly. Common wisdom among analysts is that they spend 80 percent of their time looking *for* the right data and only 20 percent of their time looking *at* the right data.

One option for ensuring that Navy analysts are better able to cope with big data is dynamically managing their workloads. Today, the Navy's intelligence specialists are, for the most part, working on "local tasks," since the allocation of tasks tends to be based on which analysts are nearby or statically assigned, rather than on who is available to accept new tasking. The main disadvantage of today's fixed, geographically based tasking arrangements is that intelligence specialists in one location can become quickly overwhelmed with tasks that need not necessarily be assigned to them but that, because of the local tasking model, come their way by default. Through modeling and simulation, we determined that tasking models that operate at the regional or global level—models in which tasks are automatically shared based on who is available to accept new tasking—outperform today's local model in terms of the productivity of imagery analysts.

Changes to how workloads are managed are not, on their own, a sufficient long-term solution to the Navy's big data challenge, however. To be complete, a solution must involve changes along all of the following four dimensions:

- people
- tools and technology
- data and data architectures
- demand and demand management.[3]

In conducting an analysis of alternatives for the Distributed Common Ground System–Navy Increment 2 (a system intended to help the Navy address the influx of data), we developed three potential alternatives. Relative to the baseline, each increases the Navy's ability to better manage and use the rising flood of ISR data. All three alternatives assume that the Navy begins to dynamically manage analysts workloads and that sensors are cued smartly.[4] S.1 describes the baseline and each of the three alternatives.

Modeling and simulation reveal that all three alternatives outperform the baseline when it comes to finding the greatest number of targets in the smallest amount of time—a performance metric that indicates how quickly a commander can be made aware of the targets around his or her area of command. This is especially true when analysts must analyze data of multiple intelligence types. In such cases, alternatives 2 and 3 vastly outperform both the baseline and alternative 1.

We recommend that the Navy pursue alternative 3 (cloud)—a strategy similar to those adopted by Google, the Intelligence Community (IC), and other large organizations grappling with big data's challenges and opportunities. Specifically, we recommend that the Navy adopt the IC's cloud approach, designing its next generation of ISR tools and systems to work with the National Security Agency's distributed cloud concept (i.e., the Intelligence Community Government Cloud). This information architecture should be sufficient to meet the

---

[3] The corresponding workflow processes are vital as well. See Isaac R. Porche III, Evan Saltzman, Roland Yardley, and Gordon Lee, "MAXINT," presentation at the Military Operations Research Workshop on Analytic Approaches to Airborne ISR, National Defense University, Ft. McNair, Washington, D.C., April 2012; and Porche et al., 2013.

[4] This means that sensors are only turned on as needed rather than being kept on continuously. Sensors cued to the target send more-relevant data and thus lower burdens on bandwidth and on analysts' cognitive reserves.

Figure S.1
The Baseline and the Three Alternatives

	Description	People	Tools and Technology	Data and Data Architecture	Demand and Demand Management
Baseline 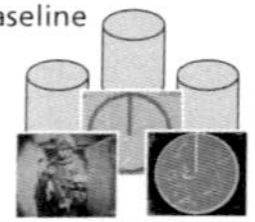	This baseline relies on current plans.	There are fewer afloat analysts. (DECREASE)	There is no change. (NO CHANGE)	There is no change in the approach to analyzing data. (NO CHANGE)	There is no change in managing personnel workflows or in managing demand for data. (NO CHANGE)
Alternative 1: Applications 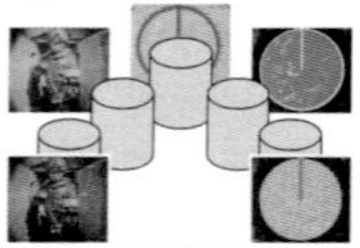	This alternative adds applications.	There are fewer afloat analysts, but there is increased reliance on reachback personnel. (REARRANGEMENT)	The Navy adds applications, including workflow-automation tools. (INCREASE APPLICATIONS)	There is no change in the approach to analyzing data. (NO CHANGE)	The Navy manages personnel workloads dynamically. Sensors are cued smartly. 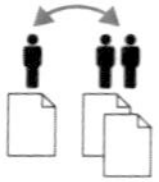
Alternative 2: Consolidation 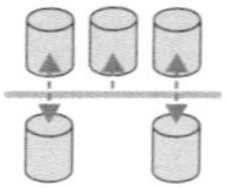	This alternative leverages an SOA (e.g., the CANES program of record).	There are fewer afloat analysts, but there is increased reliance on reachback personnel. (REARRANGEMENT)	The Navy adds more-interoperable services to enhance workflow automation. (INCREASE SERVICES)	The Navy copies the Army's approach of depending on an information clearinghouse (aka "fusion brain"). 	The Navy manages personnel workloads dynamically. Sensors are cued smartly. 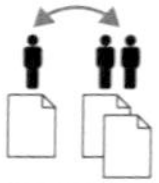
Alternative 3: Cloud 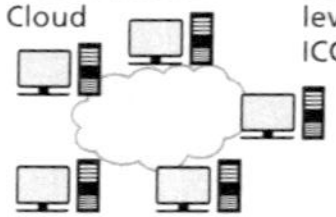	This alternative leverages ICGovCloud.	There are fewer afloat analysts, but there is increased reliance on reachback personnel. (REARRANGEMENT)	The Navy adds more services and widgets. (INCREASE SERVICES)	The Navy relies on the IC's virtual data analytic cloud.  Mini cloud node	The Navy manages personnel workloads dynamically. Sensors are cued smartly. 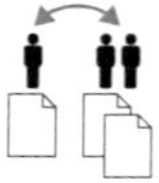

SOURCES: Screen images by Eugene Sergeev and Marcin Gardychowski via Fotolia.
NOTES: CANES = Consolidated Afloat Networks and Enterprise Services; ICGovCloud = Intelligence Community Government Cloud; SOA = service-oriented architecture.

RAND RR315-S.1

growing volumes of data that will need to be harvested and thus enable viable tasking, collection, processing, exploitation, and dissemination (TCPED) operations in the future. Integrating and leveraging an IC-developed distributed cloud architecture will enable some reachback for analysis and help analysts cope with the increasing variety and volume of data, thereby improving their ability to help commanders make better decisions.

Acknowledgments

This report draws heavily on two studies for the U.S. Navy that relied on information and plans supplied by the Navy and the Intelligence Community. We would like to thank our sponsor, OPNAV N2N6F4, and the following individuals in particular: RADM Jan Tighe, Margaret Palmieri, CAPT Jeff Myers, CAPT Vernon D. Bashaw (ret.), Debra Quigley, CDR Charles Oneil, and CDR Amy Halin. Brad Wilson, a report coauthor, developed key models and simulation tools, including models of the intelligence process that we used to analyze mission outcomes. We would like to thank Endy Min Daehner, Vernon "Ray" Koym, Matt Norton, Luis E. Reinoso, Dan Salyan, and John Yurchak, who, along with report coauthor Shane Tierney, organized a thorough data-collection process including detailed technology and risk assessments of key technologies for the cloud and other command, control, communications, computers, intelligence, surveillance, and reconnaissance systems relevant to the intelligence cycle. We would like to thank Roland Yardley, who, along with report coauthor Evan Saltzman, helped develop new manpower models that we used to factor in the productivity of the Navy's intelligence analysts. We would like to thank Jim Dryden and Stephanie Young, who provided an analysis of the economics of potential reachback locations for the Navy. We would like to thank Megan McKernan, Michelle McMullen, and Stephanie Sutton, who were instrumental in planning and hosting numerous workshops with Navy staff.

Finally, we are grateful to the reviewers Lance Menthe, Sherrill Lingel, and Cynthia Dion-Schwarz, who provided detailed feedback and suggestions on drafts of this report.

Abbreviations

BAMS	Broad Area Maritime Surveillance
BAMS-D	Broad Area Maritime Surveillance–Demonstrator
C2	command and control
CANES	Consolidated Afloat Networks and Enterprise Services
COP	common operational picture.
DCGS-N	Distributed Common Ground System–Navy
DoD	Department of Defense
IC	Intelligence Community
ICGovCloud	Intelligence Community Government Cloud
IP	Internet protocol
ISR	intelligence, surveillance, and reconnaissance
JEMA	Joint Enterprise Modeling and Analytics
LISI	levels of information systems interoperability
NATO	North Atlantic Treaty Organization
ONI	Office of Naval Intelligence
PAAT	Processing, Exploitation, and Dissemination Architecture and Analysis Tool

SOA	service-oriented architecture
STUAS	Small Tactical Unmanned Aircraft System
TCPED	tasking, collection, processing, exploitation, and dissemination
TS/SCI	Top Secret/Sensitive Compartmented Information
UAV	unmanned aerial vehicle
UCAS-D	Unmanned Combat Air System Carrier–Demonstration
UCLASS	Unmanned Carrier Launched Airborne Surveillance and Strike System
USMC STUAS	United States Marine Corps Small Tactical Unmanned Aircraft
UUV	unmanned undersea vehicle
VTUAV	vertical takeoff and landing tactical unmanned aerial vehicle

CHAPTER ONE

Big Data: Challenges and Opportunities

U.S. Navy intelligence, surveillance, and reconnaissance (ISR) functions have become critical to U.S. national security over the last two decades.[1] Within the Navy, there is a growing demand for ISR data from drones and other sources that provide situational awareness, which helps Navy vessels avoid collisions, pinpoint targets, and perform a host of other mission-critical tasks. Despite the battle-tested value of ISR systems, however, the large amount of data they generate has become overwhelming to Navy analysts. As the Intelligence Science Board wrote in 2008, referring to the entire Department of Defense (DoD), "the number of images and signal intercepts are well beyond the capacity of the existing analyst community, so there are huge backlogs for translators and image interpreters, and much of the collected data are never reviewed."[2] This is a good description of the Navy's big data challenge.

---

[1] The Joint Chiefs of Staff defines ISR as the "synchronized, integrated planning and operation of sensors, processing, exploitation and dissemination systems in direct support of current and future operations." It also states that this is "an integrated intelligence and operations function" (Joint Chiefs of Staff, *Department of Defense Dictionary of Military and Associated Terms*, November 8, 2010, as amended through July 15, 2012).

[2] Intelligence Science Board, *Integrating Sensor-Collected Intelligence*, Washington, D.C.: Office of the Under Secretary of Defense for Acquisition, Technology, and Logistics, November 2008.

What Is "Big Data"?

Although the term *big data* is popular, there is no standard definition. As the following list demonstrates, different organizations use the term to mean a wide variety of things:

- Forrester: "Techniques and technologies that make handling data at extreme scale affordable."
- Gartner: "High volume, velocity and variety information assets that demand cost-effective, innovative forms of information processing for enhanced insight and decision making."
- IBM: "More than simply a matter of size . . . an opportunity to find insights in new and emerging types of data and content, to make your business more agile, and to answer questions that were previously considered beyond your reach."
- Office of the Director of National Intelligence: "A concept to enable mass analytics within and across the data (within the confines of the security policies) to enable information integration (e.g., entity correlation)."
- McKinsey: "Datasets whose size is beyond the ability of typical database software tools to capture, store, manage, and analyze."
- Wikipedia: "A collection of data sets so large and complex that it becomes difficult to process using on-hand database management tools."
- ZDNet: "Technologies and practice of handling data sets so large that conventional database management systems cannot handle them efficiently and sometimes cannot handle them at all."[3]

In our view, *big data* is a data set so vast that it stresses the limits of traditional (i.e., relational) databases along four parameters:

- volume of data
- variety of formats, sources, and types
- velocity of searches and data retrieval
- veracity of conclusions based on data.

---

[3]   All definitions are as quoted in Office of Naval Research, "Big Data Tutorial," v1.00, slide deck, February 21, 2012.

How Big Is Big?

To understand how big "big data" is, think about the volume of information contained in the Library of Congress, one of the world's largest libraries in terms of shelf space and number of books. All of the information in the Library of Congress could be digitized into 200 terabytes, or 200 trillion bytes. Then consider the fact that the Navy currently collects the equivalent of a Library of Congress' worth of data almost every other day.[4] But even this amount is miniscule compared with the size of the entire "digital universe," which is billions of terabytes large and constantly growing.[5] Estimates of the annual growth of this universe vary, but it appears to be exponential (Figure 1.1).

The Navy's Big Data Challenge

Technically, the amount of data that can be stored by traditional databases is unlimited. However, the greater the volume of data being collected and shared, the more difficult mining, fusing, and effectively using the data in a timely manner become. In the Navy, where analysts use data to create information that informs decisionmaking, this challenge is particularly troublesome. All of the data and information collected by the Navy is potentially useful, but processing it and deriving useful knowledge from it is severely taxing the analytical capabilities

[4] Programs, Management, Analytics & Technologies, "Maritime ISR Enterprise Acquisition (MIEA) Review," white paper, January 2011. One estimate from IBM, cited by the Navy and others, is that 2.5 quintillion bytes of data (2.5×10^{18}) are created every day from public, private, and government sources (IBM, "IBM Study: Digital Era Transforming CMO's Agenda, Revealing Gap in Readiness," IBM news release, October 11, 2011).

[5] The digital universe is "every electronically stored piece of data or file" (Joe McKendrick, "Data Explosion: Enough to Fill DVDs Stretching to the Moon and Back," SmartPlanet. com, May 14, 2010b). This includes "images and videos on mobile phones uploaded to YouTube, digital movies . . . , banking data swiped [at] an ATM, security footage, subatomic collisions recorded by the Large Hadron Collider . . . , transponders recording highway tolls, voice calls . . . through digital phone lines" and much more (Data Science Series, "Digital Universe Will Grow to 40ZB in 2020, with a 62% Share for Emerging Markets," blog post, December 13, 2012).

Figure 1.1
Estimated Size of the Digital Universe

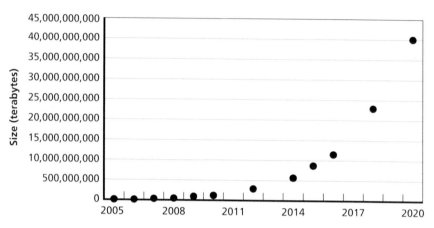

SOURCES: John Gantz, David Reinsel, Christopher Chute, Wolfgang Schlichting, John McArthur, Stephen Minton, Irida Xheneti, Anna Toncheva, and Alex Manfrediz, *The Expanding Digital Universe: A Forecast of Worldwide Information Growth Through 2010*, IDC Digital Universe Study, March 2007; John Gantz, Christopher Chute, Alex Manfrediz, Stephen Minton, David Reinsel, Wolfgang Schlichting, and Anna Toncheva, *The Diverse and Exploding Digital Universe: An Updated Forecast of Worldwide Information Growth Through 2011*, IDC Digital Universe Study, March 2008; John Gantz and David Reinsel, *As the Economy Contracts, the Digital Universe Expands*, IDC Digital Universe Study, May 2009; John Gantz and David Reinsel, *The Digital Universe Decade: Are You Ready?* IDC Digital Universe Study, May 2010; John Gantz and David Reinsel, *Extracting Value from Chaos*, IDC Digital Universe Study, June 2011; John Gantz and David Reinsel, *The Digital Universe in 2020: Big Data, Bigger Digital Shadows, and Biggest Growth in the Far East*, IDC Digital Universe Study, December 2012; Joe McKendrick, "Size of the Data Universe: 1.2 Zettabytes and Growing Fast," ZDNet.com, May 12, 2010a; Greg Miller, "MQ-4C BAMS UAS," presentation at the International Conference on Autonomous Unmanned Vehicles 2012, February 2012; Chuck Hollis, "Charting the Digital Universe: IDC's 6th Annual Study," blog post, December 11, 2012; Saroj Kar, "Less Than 1% of the World's Information Is Being Analyzed: IDC Report," *Cloud Times*, December 27, 2012.
RAND RR315-1.1

of the Navy's humans and networks. As the Navy acquires and fields new and additional sensors for collecting data, this difficulty will likely grow (Figure 1.2).

Increasingly unable to process all of its own data, the Navy has little hope—if nothing changes—of exploiting all of the potentially useful data in the greater digital universe. Commercial, government, and other sources, such as Twitter, GeoEye, Inc., and the National

Figure 1.2
The Amount of Data Increases Exponentially as the Navy Acquires New Sensors

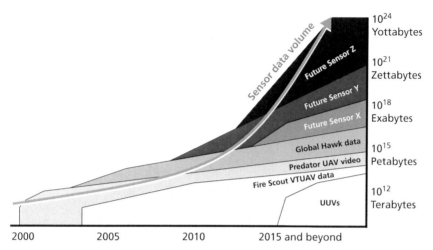

SOURCE: Programs, Management, Analytics & Technologies, 2011.
NOTES: UAV = unmanned aerial vehicle; UUV = unmanned undersea vehicle;
VTUAV = vertical takeoff and landing tactical unmanned aerial vehicle.
RAND *RR315-1.2*

Oceanic and Atmospheric Administration (to name but a few), create hundreds of terabytes of potentially useful data every day. But how much of these data can the Navy expect to make use of?

The Navy's Big Data Opportunity

ISR systems are highly valued across the military for good reasons.[6] The data they collect provide commanders with information on enemy positions and activities. They enable warfighters to locate targets with precision. They provide vital information about the location of friendly

---

[6]   In the literature, the terms *value* and *variability* have been associated with properties of big data and thus correspond to the Navy opportunities we described in the next chapter. See Yuri Demchenko, "Defining the Big Data Architecture Framework (BDAF)," presentation to the University of Amsterdam, July 14, 2013.

forces. Former U.S. Air Force intelligence lead Lt Gen David A. Deptula (ret.) has predicted that ISR will "lead in the fight" in 2020. He has also suggested that "ISR is currently moving from a supporting capability to the leading edge of national security operations."[7] As the next chapter argues, the Navy sees data collected through ISR as essential to situational awareness, which it considers a vital technological advantage. Essentially, the Navy hopes to realize the Office of the Director of National Intelligence's definition of *big data*: the enabling of "mass analytics within and across data . . . to enable information integration."

---

[7]   David Deptula, "ISR Will Lead the Fight by 2020," *Breaking Defense*, June 24, 2011.

CHAPTER TWO

What the Navy Wants from Big Data

The Navy's ISR cycle (consisting of tasking, collection, processing, exploitation, and dissemination [TCPED]) is not undertaken for its own sake but with a clear, vital objective: providing the fleet with situational awareness. In military operations, knowledge is power. In the Navy, it is situational awareness—derived, in part, from ISR data—that gives commanders that power by helping them answer four critical questions:

- Where am I?
- Where are my friends?
- Where is the enemy?
- Where is everyone else?

As the rest of this chapter demonstrates, an inability to answer any of these four questions can be disastrous.

Where Am I?

In January 2013, the USS *Guardian*, a minesweeper, ran aground in the Philippines on Tubbataha Reef, a United Nations Educational, Scientific and Cultural Organization World Heritage site (Figure 2.1). The vessel was stranded for months and, after the Navy determined it could not be recovered, was cut from the reef in three pieces and thus destroyed.

Figure 2.1
The USS *Guardian*, Stranded

SOURCE: U.S. Navy photo.
RAND *RR315-2.1*

The Navy's investigation of the incident concluded that the crew had relied on inaccurate maps and were unable to reconcile the differences between their maps of the area and more-refined coastal charts.[1] (According to another report, the National Geospatial-Intelligence Agency misplaced a reef in the Philippine Islands by eight miles on its digital nautical charts—a mistake due to "erroneous commercial satellite imagery."[2]) In sum, the crew was unable to assess the data they had in a way that would have allowed them to determine their own location with accuracy. As a result, the ship was lost, despite a costly salvage operation.

---

[1]   U.S. Pacific Fleet Public Affairs, "USS Guardian Grounding Investigation Results Released," June 20, 2013.

[2]   Bob Brewin, "How a Misplaced Reef on a Digital Chart Destroyed a Navy Minesweeper," Nextgov.com, August 5, 2013.

Where Are My Friends?

In March 2009, the USS *Hartford*, a submarine, collided with the USS *New Orleans*, an amphibious transport ship, in the Strait of Hormuz (Figure 2.2). Fifteen sailors were injured, thousands of gallons of diesel were spilled, and $100 million in damage was done.[3] A senior Navy officer attributed part of the blame to analysts' inability to discern among a number of radar contacts: "There were a whole lot of watchstanders that failed to recognize the sensor data presented to them."[4]

Figure 2.2
The Aftermath of the USS *New Orleans* and USS *Hartford* Collision

SOURCE: U.S. Navy photo by CDR Jane Campbell.
RAND *RR315-2.2*

---

[3] "U.S. Navy Vessels in Bahrain for Evaluation After Collision," CNN.com, March 21, 2009.

[4] Andrew Scutro, "Admiral: Complacency Caused Sub Collision," *Navy Times*, October 29, 2009.

Where Is the Enemy?

In October 2000, the USS *Cole*, a guided-missile destroyer, was attacked in the port of Aden in Yemen. Terrorists pulled a small boat to the vessel's side and waved and smiled at the crew before detonating explosives that created a 40-foot by 40-foot hole in the destroyer's hull, killing 17 sailors and injuring 39 others (Figure 2.3). The attack on the USS *Cole*, the deadliest against a U.S. naval vessel since the USS *Stark* came under fire during the Iran-Iraq War in May 1987,[5] may be one of the most well known examples of the importance of knowing the enemy's location.

Figure 2.3
The Attack on the USS *Cole*

SOURCE: Department of Defense photo by Sgt. Don L. Maes, U.S. Marine Corps.
RAND *RR315-2.3*

---

[5] 9/11 Memorial, "USS Cole Bombing," web page, undated.

Where Is Everyone Else?

Awareness of commercial shipping traffic and other vessels that are nei-
ther friends nor enemies is also critical. In August 2012, the USS *Porter*,
a destroyer, collided with a commercial oil tanker in the middle of
the night in the Strait of Hormuz (Figure 2.4). The exact cause of the
collision has not yet been reported in open sources, but audio from
the bridge of the USS *Porter* suggests that navigation errors may have
played a significant role. Improved situational awareness might have
prevented this mishap.

Figure 2.4
The USS *Porter* Collision

SOURCE: U.S. Navy photo by Mass Communication Specialist 3rd Class
Jonathan Sunderman.
RAND *RR315-2.4*

Situational Awareness: A Vital Goal

As the examples provided in this chapter demonstrate, situational awareness is critical to naval operations, and the Navy needs to improve its ability to make sense of the data that growing numbers, and growing varieties, of sensors provide. Indeed, as the Intelligence Science Board reported in 2008, "integrating data from different sensors and platforms" could "dramatically enhance" geolocation and other important tasks.[6] So what, exactly, is preventing the Navy from reaping the benefits of ISR-provided data? The next chapter argues that two main factors are at play.

---

[6] Intelligence Science Board, 2008.

CHAPTER THREE

Barriers to Benefiting from Big Data

As we have argued in previous chapters, today's ISR capabilities have the potential to enhance the state of naval situational awareness. However, the Navy needs to improve its ability to make sense of the data being collected. In particular, it faces two challenges: timely consumption and accurate integration.

Timely Consumption

In 2020, there could be twice as many fielded unmanned ISR platforms and related sensors as there are today in early 2014 (Figure 3.1). One such platform is the MQ-4C Triton, a UAV developed under the Broad Area Maritime Surveillance (BAMS) program and designed to fly surveillance missions of up to 24 hours at altitudes of more than 10 miles (Figure 3.2).[1] Existing and emerging unmanned platforms will join a host of manned platforms (including the P-8 Poseidon, shown in Figure 3.3) and national assets (a variety of monitoring technologies known as *National Technical Means*) that carry sensor packages. Each of these platforms is capable of generating enormous amounts of data in a single mission or day. For example, the Office of Naval Research reported in 2012 that a BAMS UAV can collect 10–20 terabytes per mission.[2]

---

[1] Naval Air Systems Command Public Affairs, "Navy Triton Unmanned Aircraft System Completes First Flight," story number NNS130522-20, 2013.

[2] Office of Naval Research, 2012. These numbers are likely to be even larger in the future.

Figure 3.1
Anticipated Growth in UAV Sensor Platforms

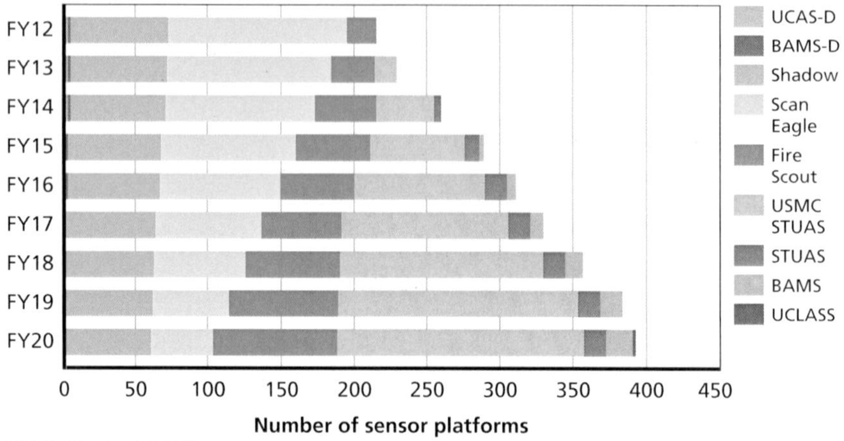

SOURCE: Card, 2012.
NOTE: BAMS = Broad Area Maritime Surveillance; BAMS-D Broad Area Maritime Surveillance System–Demonstrator; STUAS = Small Tactical Unmanned Aircraft System; UCAS-D = Unmanned Combat Air System Carrier–Demonstration; UCLASS = Unmanned Carrier Launched Airborne Surveillance and Strike System; USMC STUAS = United States Marine Corps Small Tactical Unmanned Aircraft. Additional information on these platforms can be found in Porche et al., 2013.
RAND RR315-3.1

Unfortunately, much of the data collected by ISR platforms never reaches the analysts who need to see it—in fact, as little as 5 percent may be getting through. In the case of analysts working afloat on ships, a large part of the problem is extremely slow download times caused by bandwidth and connectivity limitations. Whereas an ashore analyst working with a 100-gigabits-per-second transfer speed can download a terabyte of data in four minutes, an afloat analyst working with a 40-megabits-per-second transfer speed needs three days to do so (Table 3.1).

Compounding the download-time challenge are two additional factors. First, the communications pipelines used by the analysts are sometimes outside their control. For example, access to a satellite communications channel may be shared with others and, based on regional or national priorities, may be unavailable for a Navy analyst's use. Second, analysts must often download multiple pieces of large data

Figure 3.2
The MQ-4C Triton UAV

SOURCE: U.S. Navy photo, courtesy of Northrop Grumman.
RAND *RR315-3.2*

Figure 3.3
The P-8 Poseidon

SOURCE: U.S. Navy photo.
RAND *RR315-3.3*

Table 3.1
Download Times for One Terabyte

Service	Max Transfer Speed (in bits per second)	Download Time in Seconds	Download Time in Minutes	Download Time in Hours	Download Time in Days
100-gigabits-per-second service	40,000,000,000	220	4	NA	NA
40-gigabits-per-second service	16,000,000,000	550	9	NA	NA
Large Data 10-gigabits-per second Joint Capability Technology Demonstration[a]	8,500,000,000	1,035	17	NA	NA
10-gigabits-per-second service	4,000,000,000	2,199	37	<1	NA
155-megabits-per-second service	62,000,000	141,872	2,365	39	2
50-megabits-per-second Wideband Global Satellite communications channel[b]	40,000,000	212,902	3,665	61	3

SOURCE: Programs, Management, Analytics & Technologies, 2011.

[a] The Large Data Joint Capability Technology Demonstration researched bandwidth efficiency in order to support large transfers of data.

[b] A 50-megabit-per-second Wideband Global Satellite communications channel is a dedicated satellite communications channel used by afloat analysts.

(such as high-resolution images) to find exactly what they need. This is because many of the large pieces of data generated by ISR sensors (including imagery, video, and audio) are "untagged," meaning that they are unaccompanied by information that would help analysts find them and decide whether to access them. Demand management, discussed in Chapter Five, could alleviate some of the burden on analysts, but, in cases where data cannot be tagged, the raw images must be downloaded, and slow download times once again come into play. In sum, most of the time, analysts do not have the luxury of receiving the "right" data in a timely fashion.

Accurate Integration

Navy analysts are confronted with a wide variety of data streaming in from different ISR platforms and sensors—data they must integrate to ensure accurate, comprehensive situational awareness. As Figure 3.4 shows, these data come from multiple types of intelligence sources. To access and make sense of the data, many analysts sit at workstations comprising multiple screens, each showing different streams of data and each loaded with different suites of tools (Figure 3.5). In many

Figure 3.4
Diverse Data Sources

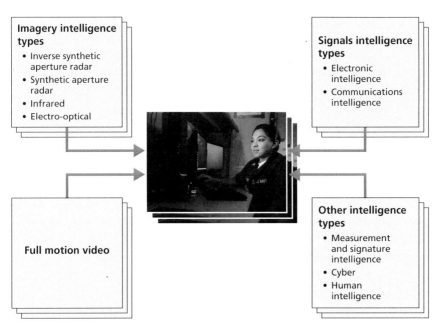

SOURCE: U.S. Navy photo by Mass Communication Specialist 3rd Class Brooks B. Patton Jr.

RAND *RR315-3.4*

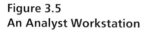

Figure 3.5
An Analyst Workstation

SOURCE: U.S. Navy photo by Mass Communication Specialist Seaman
K. Cecelia Engrums.
RAND RR315-3.5

cases, the applications, databases, and operating systems underlying
these tools are produced by different vendors and are not interoperable.
Sailors told us that they are overwhelmed as they struggle to master the
functions provided by each tool in the suite at their workstations. The
ability to fuse multiple intelligence types in a timely manner is a known
gap that the Distributed Common Ground System–Navy (DCGS-N)
Increment 2 program of record is required to close.

A second challenge is the existence of multiple and often mutu-
ally exclusive security domains (Figure 3.6). Some ISR platforms are
designed to feed all of their data into a specific database that resides in a
specific, isolated security domain, regardless of whether all of the individual pieces of data collected by that platform really need to be classi-
fied at that particular level. Some specific databases (and, by extension,
the data contained within them) are accessible only through a specific
network, meaning that it is possible for a Secret-level piece of data to
reside in a Top Secret–level database that is accessible only through a
Top Secret network. For analysts, this means that searching for a single

Figure 3.6
Security Domains Today

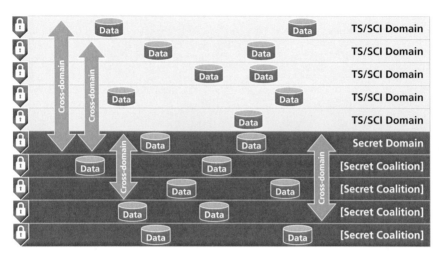

SOURCE: Office of Naval Research, 2012.
NOTE: TS/SCI = Top Secret/Sensitive Compartmented Information.
RAND RR315-3.6

piece of data can require them to use multiple networks to access multiple databases—a dampener on productivity and a dangerous situation, given that achieving accurate situational awareness requires integrating data from multiple sources in a timely fashion.

We know from a study of the Afghan Mission Network, which was used during Operation Enduring Freedom, that improved collaboration can occur when the number of security domains is reduced.[3] One approach to enabling the consolidation of security domains is found in

---

[3]   Chad C. Serena, Isaac R. Porche III, Joel B. Predd, Jan Osburg, and Bradley Lossing, *Lessons Learned from the Afghan Mission Network: Developing a Coalition Contingency Network*, Santa Monica, Calif.: RAND Corporation, forthcoming. The Afghan Mission Network enabled the United States and its allies in Afghanistan to subsume

their own internal secret communications networks in favor of a common network for managing command and control and sharing intelligence, surveillance and reconnaissance information. . . . [T]o implement the Afghanistan Mission Network, which creates a common operating picture for all U.S. and NATO [North Atlantic Treaty Organization] commanders in Afghanistan, the U.S. military had to undergo a shift in the way it manages its Secret IP [Internet Protocol] Router Network. (Barry Rosenberg, the Apache Accumulo project (previously called Cloudbase) incubated by the National Security Agency. Apache Accumulo facilitates security domain consolidation by allowing cell-level security-tagging mechanisms for database entries. Essentially, this means that each piece of data in the database is tagged with its specific classification level. Once this information is present, access-control techniques can be used to limit or grant access to that piece of data based on a user's security credentials.[4] In the Navy, the progression to a single security domain might look something like Figure 3.7. Ultimately, the goal would be to create a single network domain that provides access to data at multiple levels of security classification.

How Analysts Cope Today

We have shown that Navy analysts are struggling with the timely consumption and accurate integration of big data, and we expect their challenges to grow as the Navy fields new and additional ISR platforms. Common wisdom among analysts themselves is that they spend 80 percent of their time looking *for* the right data and only 20 percent of their time looking *at* the right data. Unfortunately, our modeling

---

"Battlefield Network Connects Allied Forces in Afghanistan," DefenseSystems.com, September 14, 2010)

[4] For more information, see Paul Burkhardt and Chris Waring, "An NSA Big Graph Experiment," presentation at the Carnegie Mellon University SDI/ISTC Seminar, Pittsburgh, Pa., May 20, 2013; Jeremy Kepner, Christian Anderson, William Arcand, David Bestor, Bill Bergeron, Chansup Byun, Matthew Hubbell, Peter Michaleas, Julie Mullen, David O'Gwynn, Andrew Prout, Albert Reuther, Antonio Rosa, and Charles Yee, "D4M 2.0 Schema: A General Purpose High Performance Schema for the Accumulo Database," paper presented at the 2013 IEEE High Performance Extreme Computing Conference, September 12, 2013; Office of Naval Research, 2012; Isaac R. Porche III, Bradley Wilson, Shane Tierney, Ray Koym, James Dryden, Evan Saltzman, Roland J. Yardley, John M. Yurchak, Stephanie Young, Endy M. Daehner, Megan McKernan, and Kate Giglio, *The DCGS-Navy Increment 2 Analysis of Alternatives: Options for Meeting the TCPED Challenges and Opportunities*, Santa Monica, Calif.: RAND Corporation, 2013; and Jaikumar Vijayan, "Facebook Moves 30-Petabyte Hadoop Cluster to New Data Center," *ComputerWorld*, July 29, 2011.

Figure 3.7
Security Domains in the Future?

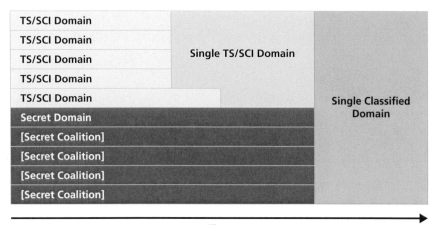

SOURCE: U.S. Department of the Navy, 2012.
RAND *RR315-3.7*

and simulation found evidence to support this split.[5] The truth is that analysts are drowning in data, and the Navy has limits on the number of analysts it employs. So, how can the Navy ensure that the analysts it does employ are better able to cope with big data? The next chapter explores one option: dynamically managing analyst workloads.

---

[5] See Isaac R. Porche III, Evan Saltzman, Roland Yardley, and Gordon Lee, "MAXINT," presentation at the Military Operations Research Workshop on Analytic Approaches to Airborne ISR, National Defense University, Ft. McNair, Washington, D.C., April 2012; and Porche et al., 2013.

CHAPTER FOUR

Dynamically Managing Analyst Workloads

Compared with the other military services, the Navy employs only a small number of analysts. As of 2011, there were several thousand Navy analysts divided among five intelligence specialties (Figure 4.1). It is important to understand that, despite the anticipated growth in incoming data, the Navy will not increase the number of analysts (including intelligence specialists) that it employs. It is also important

Figure 4.1
Approximate Number of Navy Intelligence Specialists as of 2011

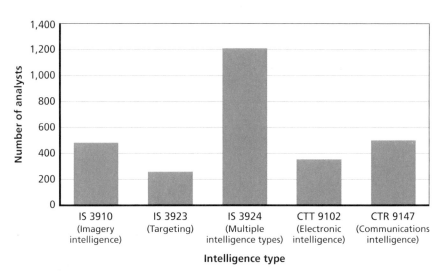

NOTE: A description of the tasks performed by these analysts is provided in Porche et al., 2013.

RAND RR315-4.1

to understand that the Navy's analysts are spread around the world: in the Navy's reachback intelligence center, in maritime operations centers, and afloat on ships (Figure 4.2). They are located both in the United States and abroad, both afloat and ashore, working on large-deck ships and "small boys" (e.g., destroyers, cruisers).

One potential way to increase analyst productivity is to physically locate Navy analysts together. However, RAND modeling, based on a year of operational data, showed that the physical location of Navy intelligence specialists is not necessarily the deciding factor in their productivity.[1] A dynamically balanced workload appears to be much more important.

Today's Navy intelligence specialists are, for the most part, working on "local tasks," since the allocation of tasks tends to be based on which analysts are nearby or statically assigned, rather than on who is available globally to accept new tasking. In the main, today's tasking

Figure 4.2
Navy Intelligence Specialists Are Distributed Globally

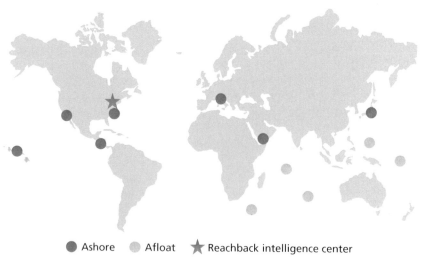

● Ashore   ● Afloat   ★ Reachback intelligence center

NOTE: Some locations are notional.
RAND RR315-4.2

---

[1]   Details are in Porche et al., 2013.

arrangements are fixed and separated based on geography (Figure 4.3; for more-detailed drawings of the tasking arrangements, see Figure A.1).[2] The main disadvantage of this arrangement is that intelligence specialists in one location can become quickly overwhelmed with tasks that need not necessarily be assigned to them but that, because of the local tasking model, come their way by default.

What if the Navy were to consider implementing a regional (Figure 4.4) or even global (Figure 4.5) tasking model instead? In these models, tasks would be automatically shared and allocated within regions (or, in the latter case, globally) based on who is available to accept new tasking. RAND researchers developed a model of intelligence specialist productivity and, using a year of operational data, found that the regional and global tasking models do indeed improve

Figure 4.3
Today's Tasking Arrangements Are "Local"

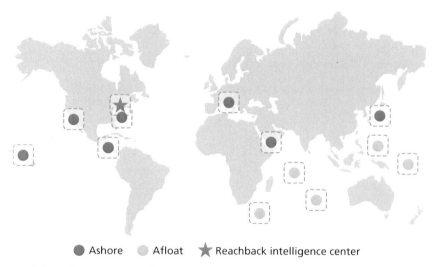

● Ashore   ● Afloat   ★ Reachback intelligence center

NOTE: Some locations are notional.
RAND RR315-4.3

---

[2]   This is not universally true, however: In the case of some intelligence types, there is some reachback to analysts at the Navy's reachback intelligence center or maritime operations centers.

Figure 4.4
Tomorrow's Tasking Arrangements Could Be "Regional"

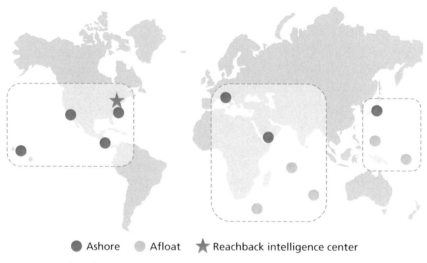

<table>
<tr><td>● Ashore</td><td>● Afloat</td><td>★ Reachback intelligence center</td></tr>
</table>

NOTE: Some locations are notional.

RAND RR315-4.4

Figure 4.5
Tomorrow's Tasking Arrangements Could Be "Global"

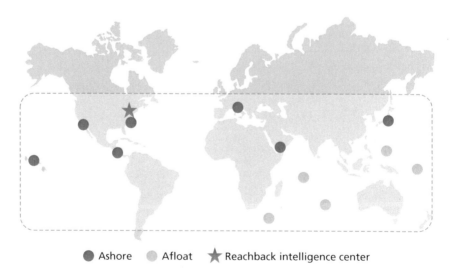

<table>
<tr><td>● Ashore</td><td>● Afloat</td><td>★ Reachback intelligence center</td></tr>
</table>

NOTE: Some locations are notional.

RAND RR315-4.5

intelligence specialist productivity. However, this is true only to a certain extent.

Figure 4.6 shows, at an abstracted level, how intelligence specialist productivity changes based on the tasking model. In this case, we are considering the productivity of imagery analysts processing data coming from a Navy BAMS UAV. The y-axis measures how often an imagery analyst processes data in time to satisfy a customer (for instance, a ship commander), which decreases from top to bottom. The x-axis shows the number of BAMS UAV orbits, which increases from left to right. As the figure shows, regional tasking outperforms local tasking, and global tasking outperforms both. However, as the number of BAMS UAV orbits increases—as we know it will—all three models eventually dip down, revealing that imagery analysts simply will not be able to keep up with all of the imagery coming their way, no matter how we balance their workloads.

Implementing a regional or global tasking model might buy the Navy a short-term improvement in analyst productivity, but changes to how workloads are managed are not, on their own, a viable long-term solution. The next chapter examines more-comprehensive alternatives to solving the big data challenge.

Figure 4.6
Modeling Results: Imagery Analysts (Abstracted)

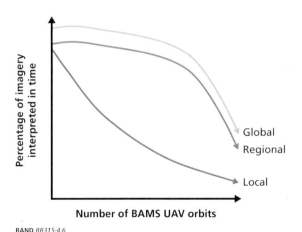

CHAPTER FIVE

Alternatives for Dealing with Big Data

We have shown that better management of analyst workloads is not a sufficient or long-term solution to the Navy's big data challenge.[1] To be complete, a solution must involve changes along all of the following four dimensions:

- people
- tools and technology
- data and data architectures
- demand and demand management.

This chapter presents alternatives for dealing with big data, beginning with a description of the baseline scenario.

Baseline

Currently, Navy analysts must access data that are stored in a number of discrete, unconnected databases (Figure 5.1; for more-detailed drawings of the baseline and alternatives, see Figure A.2).[2] To do this, they must master and use many different desktop applications. To gain awareness of the existence and location of data they might need, they must communicate with other analysts through such tools as email, chat software, and telephone calls. They face several challenges as

---

[1] It may be necessary, but is not sufficient.

[2] Note that this challenge applies to all of the services, not just the Navy.

Figure 5.1
Baseline

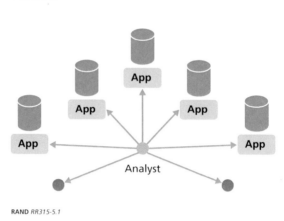

Analyst

they download, assess, and make sense of raw data. For instance, as explained in Chapter Three, download times are often quite slow, especially afloat. Collaboration and integration generally take place manually rather than in an automated fashion. Many different data types need to be integrated.

People. In the baseline scenario, the Navy does not increase the number of analysts it employs. (In fact, the number of afloat analysts decreases in both the baseline and all of the alternatives.) In general, Navy analysts in the baseline scenario continue to work on tasking that is developed and assigned locally or in accordance with static, fixed arrangements. There are some fixed work-sharing arrangements,[3] but there is no dynamic, real-time tasking of exploitation or other tasks.

Tools and technology. The current architecture and environment continue to set limits on developers' ability to easily incorporate new tools or systems because there is no service-oriented architecture (SOA) or application-integration framework that simplifies the process of adding new applications.[4]

---

[3] This includes so-called imagery federations.

[4] An SOA is an architectural style. Simply described, it is an architecture consisting of service providers and service consumers that enables business agility through the use of loosely coupled services. Services are implementation-independent reusable business functions that

Data and database architecture. In the baseline scenario, numerous stovepiped datasets and numerous security domains persist. The result is a level of system interoperability that is marginal. "Connected interoperability" exists, but mostly between homogeneous systems. Manual exchanges are still required. Databases remain separated, each relying on traditional relational databases that support separate applications, separate services, and separate catalogs. The environment scores poorly (a "1") on the levels of information systems interoperability (LISI) scale shown in Table 5.1.

Demand management. For the purposes of analysis, the baseline scenario and all three alternatives assume a judicious collection of intelligence. For example, sensors are smartly cued to targets, meaning that sensors are turned on only as needed rather than left on continuously. Sensors cued to the target send more-relevant data and thus lower burdens on bandwidth and on analysts' cognitive reserves.

Alternative 1: Applications (Adding More Tools to the Baseline)

We call the first alternative to the baseline the *applications* alternative because one of its primary enhancements relative to the baseline is to add more applications to analyst workstations (Figure 5.2). This aims to help analysts take advantage of the increased variety of data afforded by the proliferation of data types and databases. It does not represent any significant design or development activities relative to the baseline but rather adds current and emerging DoD and Intelligence Community (IC) tools to address specific identified capability gaps.

People. As in the baseline scenario, the Navy does not increase the number of analysts it employs. However, alternatives 1, 2, and 3

---

are discovered as self-describing interfaces and invoked using open-standard protocols across networks (Isaac R. Porche III, James Dryden, Kathryn Connor, Bradley Wilson, Shawn McKay, Kate Giglio, and Juan Montelibano, *Finding Services for an Open Architecture: A Review of Existing Applications and Programs in PEO C4I*, Santa Monica, Calif.: RAND Corporation, MG-1071-NAVY, 2011). SOA principles enable developers to aggregate and abstract interfaces, thereby reducing the number of interfaces required.

Table 5.1
Levels of Information Systems Interoperability Scale

Level	Description	Information Exchange
Level 4: Enterprise	Interactive manipulation; shared data and applications	Distributed global information and applications; simultaneous interactions with complex data; advanced collaboration (e.g., interactive COP update); event-triggered global database
Level 3: Domain	Shared data; "separate" applications	Shared databases; sophisticated collaboration (e.g., COP)
Level 2: Functional	Minimal common functions; separate data and applications	Heterogeneous product exchange; basic collaboration; group collaboration (e.g., exchange of annotated imagery, maps with overlays)
Level 1: Connected	Electronic connection; separate data and applications	Homogeneous product exchange (e.g., voice, tactical data links, text files, transfers, messages, email)
Level 0: Isolated	Not connected	Manual gateway (e.g., diskette, tape, hard-copy exchange)

SOURCE: Adapted from C4ISR Architectures Working Group, "Levels of Information Systems Interoperability (LISI)," 1998, Figure 2-5.
NOTE: COP = common operational picture.

involve greater usage of ashore analysts—an arrangement known as *reachback*[5]—relative to the baseline (although afloat analytic capabilities are maintained). They also assume that the Navy chooses to dynamically manage analyst workflow (either regionally or globally). The motivation for this shift is rooted in decades-old initiatives to manage DoD end-strength.[6]

---

[5]   Reachback is the "process of obtaining products, services, and applications, or forces, or equipment, or material from organizations that are not forward deployed" (Joint Chiefs of Staff, 2012).

[6]   In 2003, then–Secretary of Defense Donald Rumsfeld exhorted the military services to explore options to reduce the footprint of forward-deployed forces in an effort to reduce "both the number of forces deployed as well as the rotation base multiple needed to maintain that number of troops forward-deployed" (U.S. Secretary of Defense, "Action Agenda to Support 'End Strength' Memo Tasks," memorandum, August 25, 2003).

Figure 5.2
Alternative 1: Applications

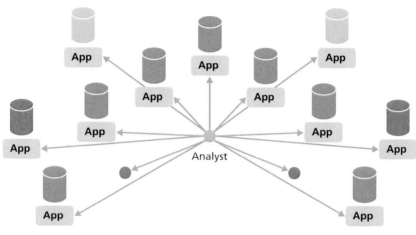

RAND *RR315-5.2*

Tools and technology. The Navy adds applications as discrete modules to address a number of existing capability gaps. These applications provide analysts with the additional capabilities they need to exploit the volume and variety of imagery and other sensor data coming from UAVs and other sources that support maritime domain awareness.

Data and architecture. The Navy adopts software that enables more interoperability (specifically, a functional interoperability that helps heterogeneous applications exchange data).[7] This is a slight improvement over the baseline, scoring a "2" on the LISI scale.

Demand management. For the purposes of analysis, the baseline scenario and all three alternatives assume a judicious collection of intelligence.

---

[7] An example of this software is the Joint Enterprise Modeling and Analytics (JEMA) tool. JEMA, developed by the National Security Agency, is used by analysts in the IC. It runs in windows and allows users to record and save workflows (e.g., "keystrokes" for accessing, preparing, and manipulating data) as executables that can be reused and repeated.

Alternative 2: Consolidation (Adopt a Service-Oriented Environment)

We call the second alternative to the baseline the *consolidation* alternative because it primarily concerns itself with consolidation of applications and their corresponding data and databases (Figure 5.3). This alternative is built around an SOA,[8] which can host web services that can be built to run within a common browser and shared with partners in other agencies and services. The idea is to move away from the development of separate applications and to enable many different analysts to access capabilities more broadly. This alternative represents

Figure 5.3
Alternative 2: Consolidation

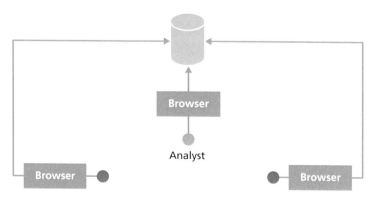

NOTE: This figure shows the consolidation that can be accomplished at the user-interface level (via browser). We do not mean to imply that browsers are necessarily directly connected to data without some intermediary capability (such as an analytic engine).
RAND *RR315-5.3*

---

[8]   The Navy's Consolidated Afloat Networks and Enterprise Services (CANES) program of record intends to provide a shipboard SOA along with the ability to host shared software services. CANES is touted as the Navy's "next generation of networks and computing infrastructure, primarily for use on ships. The system consists of hardware, operating systems, virtualization software, system management software, and numerous applications" (Jessie Riposo, John Gordon IV, Robert Murphy, Bradley Wilson, and Isaac R. Porche III, *CANES Contracting Strategies for Full Deployment*, Santa Monica, Calif.: RAND Corporation, TR-993-NAVY, 2012).

significant design and development geared toward the integration of new and existing tools, enabling a high level of interoperability.[9] Multi-intelligence fusion and end-to-end workflow automation result.

People. As in the baseline scenario, the Navy does not increase the number of analysts it employs. However, alternatives 1, 2, and 3 employ greater usage of ashore analysts relative to the baseline. They also assume that the Navy chooses to dynamically manage analyst workflow.

Tools and technology. Capability is provided by software in the form of web services and widgets that bridge identified gaps.[10] The number of interfaces required is equal to or less than the number of interfaces required in either alternative 1 or the baseline scenario.

Data and architecture. This consolidation alternative assumes a high level of interoperability specifically enabled by an open architecture (for applications) and a fusion brain (for the data).[11] This improvement scores a "3" on the LISI scale.

Demand management. For the purposes of analysis, the baseline scenario and all three alternatives assume a judicious collection of intelligence.

Alternative 3: Cloud (Join the Distributed Cloud)

The third and final alternative moves data, databases, applications, widgets, services, and other elements into a cloud architecture (Figure 5.4). Used generally, the term *cloud* refers to many different ways of sharing data, tools, or computers. In this report, we are referring to a specific cloud architecture being developed by the IC: a cloud of clouds called

---

[9] These include tools to accommodate Maritime Domain Awareness capability needs.

[10] A widget is an application or interface component that enables a user to perform a function or access a service.

[11] This open architecture could be enabled in a number of ways (e.g., use of an enterprise service bus, development of an application integration framework that facilitates scalability with respect to the number of interfacing applications). This would alleviate the need for pair-wise interconnections between separate tools.

Figure 5.4
Alternative 3: Cloud

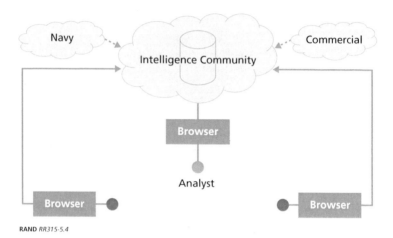

the Intelligence Community Government Cloud (ICGovCloud).[12] Compared with alternative 2, which relies on consolidation that is largely physical, alternative 3 is virtual consolidation enabled by the cloud computing concept and its associated architecture.

People. As in the baseline scenario, the Navy does not increase the number of analysts it employs. However, alternatives 1, 2, and 3 employ greater usage of ashore analysts relative to the baseline. They also assume that the Navy chooses to dynamically manage analyst workflow.

Tools and technology. Capability is provided by a cloud architecture that enables development of web services and widgets that bridge identified gaps. Once again, the number of interfaces required is equal to or less than the number of interfaces required in either alternative 1 or the baseline scenario.

Data and architecture. Alternative 3 results in the highest level of interoperability relative to all other options, scoring a "4" on the LISI

---

[12] This includes "mini-clouds" both afloat and ashore and of different types (e.g., a data cloud, a utility cloud, a storage cloud) (Greg Shaffer, "It's All About the Data," presentation to the Armed Forces Communications and Electronics Association, August 21, 2012). For further details, see Porche et al., 2013.

scale. The architecture is IC-driven and leverages that infrastructure and those tools to the greatest extent.

The Navy is currently exploring the use of cloud technology to ingest, store, and exploit its organic (i.e., onboard) sensor data. One vision for this technology is that all organic sensor data are ingested and then forwarded, on demand, to shore-based clouds. This would enable distributed alerting and analytics initiated by strategic and tactical users. The goal is to exponentially increase the operational relevance of remotely collected sensor data. These data would be discoverable and forwarded on a per-request basis.[13]

Advantages and Disadvantages of the Alternatives

Alternative 1 (applications) is designed to help analysts take advantage of the increased variety of data afforded by the proliferation of data types and databases. However, adding applications to workstations could have the effect of complicating an analyst's job rather than streamlining it. Desktop and workflow automation tools could help mitigate these complications.

Alternative 2 (consolidation) results in the physical colocation of diverse data, thereby enabling the consolidation of tools. Under this alternative, an analyst would likely need to master fewer interfaces than in alternative 1 or the baseline. However, a certain amount of raw data would still be passed to and from the consolidation point. (The Army used this approach in Afghanistan, calling it the *Fusion Brain*.[14])

Alternative 3 (cloud) results in the virtual collation of diverse data, leveraging IC tools, infrastructure, and data to a greater degree than the other alternatives. It relies on a data strategy that includes the

---

[13] A small Navy program known as "ISR Lite" demonstrated that it is possible to extend a cloud to lower-echelon "edge" forces, including those afloat (Shaffer, 2012).

[14] See Porche et al., 2013.

use of metadata and the adoption of a common metadata catalog.[15] Clouds exist afloat and ashore.

Differences Among the Baseline and the Alternatives

Table 5.2 describes differences among the baseline and the alternatives in four areas: data-sharing operational concept, security domains, workflow, and data flow.[16]

Summary of the Baseline and Alternatives

Figure 5.5 summarizes the baseline and alternatives, showing effects on the four dimensions listed at the beginning of this chapter. (See Table A.1 for additional descriptions along other dimensions.) Our analysis of the baseline and alternatives—including their relative performance, cost, and risk—follows in Chapter Six.

---

[15] Metadata are data about data. In the context of ISR, metadata associated with a piece of raw data might include such information as what type of data it is (e.g., video, audio), where it was collected, when it was collected, and how large it is. The Intelligence Science Board (2008) recommends that metadata tagging of sensor-collected data be undertaken and that it be done as close to the sensor as possible.

[16] RAND identified these four areas of importance during conversations with analysts, during modeling, and during the study described in Porche et al., 2013.

Table 5.2
Differences Among the Baseline and the Alternatives

Alternative	Data-Sharing Operational Concept	Security Domains	Workflow	Data Flow
Baseline	Stovepiped relational databases are accessed locally and remotely.	Multiple security domains persist. Data are exchanged across them using guards (e.g., Radiant Mercury).	Analysts access data stored in unconnected databases using a variety of applications involving many steps.	Raw and exploited data flow into sometimes isolated, site-specific databases (i.e., stovepipes).
Alternative 1: Applications	Stovepiped relational databases are accessed locally and remotely.	Multiple security domains persist. Data are exchanged across them using guards (e.g., Radiant Mercury).	Automation tools help streamline analyst workflow, reducing the number of steps required.	Raw and exploited data flow into sometimes isolated, site-specific databases (i.e., stovepipes).
Alternative 2: Consolidation	A "fusion brain" stores feeds from various data sources, serving as a robust information clearinghouse in a small number of relational databases.	The number of domains is reduced to two: Secret and Top Secret.	Interoperability, data consolidation, and automation tools help streamline analyst workflow, further reducing the number of steps required.	Raw and exploited data are inserted into "brains" located in and outside the continental United States.
Alternative 3: Cloud	ICGovCloud stores metadata in a virtual data analytic cloud.	There is a single, consolidated classified security domain.	Interoperability, automation tools, and cloud-related advantages result in the smallest number of steps required.	Data are ingested and tagged at the source. Metadata are shared with local and IC clouds. Raw data are shared only upon request.

Figure 5.5
Summary of the Baseline and Alternatives

	Description	People	Tools and Technology	Data and Data Architecture	Demand and Demand Management
Baseline 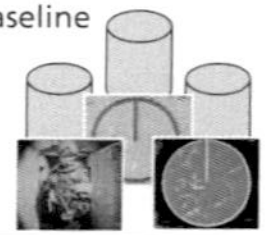	This baseline relies on current plans.	There are fewer afloat analysts. (DECREASE)	There is no change. (NO CHANGE)	There is no change in the approach to analyzing data. (NO CHANGE)	There is no change in managing personnel workflows or in managing demand for data. (NO CHANGE)
Alternative 1: Applications 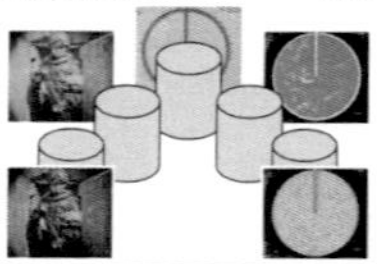	This alternative adds applications.	There are fewer afloat analysts, but there is increased reliance on reachback personnel. (REARRANGEMENT)	The Navy adds applications, including workflow-automation tools. (INCREASE APPLICATIONS)	There is no change in the approach to analyzing data. (NO CHANGE)	The Navy manages personnel workloads dynamically. Sensors are cued smartly. 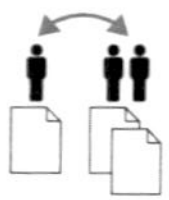
Alternative 2: Consolidation 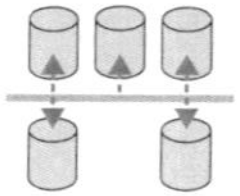	This alternative leverages an SOA (e.g., the CANES program of record).	There are fewer afloat analysts, but there is increased reliance on reachback personnel. (REARRANGEMENT)	The Navy adds more-interoperable services to enhance workflow automation. (INCREASE SERVICES)	The Navy copies the Army's approach of depending on an information clearinghouse (aka "fusion brain"). 	The Navy manages personnel workloads dynamically. Sensors are cued smartly. 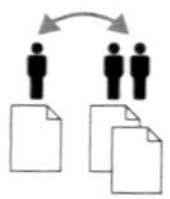
Alternative 3: Cloud 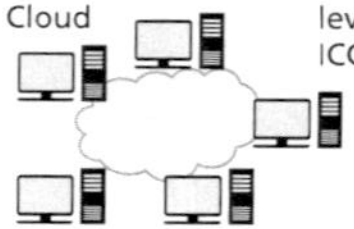	This alternative leverages ICGovCloud.	There are fewer afloat analysts, but there is increased reliance on reachback personnel. (REARRANGEMENT)	The Navy adds more services and widgets. (INCREASE SERVICES)	The Navy relies on the IC's virtual data analytic cloud. 	The Navy manages personnel workloads dynamically. Sensors are cued smartly. 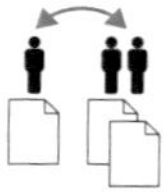

Mini cloud node

SOURCES: Screen images by Eugene Sergeev and Marcin Gardychowski via Fotolia.

CHAPTER SIX
Analysis

In this chapter, we evaluate the baseline and the three alternatives in terms of their relative performance, cost, and risk.

Performance

Using modeling and simulation tools to quantitatively measure performance differences among the alternatives,[1] and considering multiple operational missions and force structures, we determined the following for the baseline and each alternative:

- How many sensor platforms can be handled?
- What volume of data can be exchanged?
- How much electronic imagery can be analyzed in a sufficiently timely fashion?
- How many intelligence types can be fused?
- How many targets can be identified using multiple types of intelligence?

One useful performance metric is how quickly a commander can be made aware of the targets around his or her area of command.

---

[1] The bulk of our modeling and simulation work was conducted in the RAND-developed Processing, Exploitation, and Dissemination Architecture and Analysis Tool (PAAT). This tool has broad applicability for exploring the flow of intelligence information within the context of a mission. One of PAAT's key innovations is its ability to simulate intelligence specialist workflows at a level that represents their specific tasks.

Figure 6.1 shows, at an abstracted level, what percentage of targets are found across time, given data of a single intelligence type. The baseline is the least effective, resulting in the lowest percentage of targets found. Alternatives 1, 2, and 3 outperform the baseline, with alternative 3 (cloud) resulting in the greatest number of targets found most quickly.

Figure 6.2 shows, again at an abstracted level, what percentage of targets are found across time, given data of multiple intelligence types. In this case, analysts are fusing data from two or more different kinds of intelligence sources—a process that, as we explained in Chapter Three, improves the accuracy or "veracity" of the commander's situational awareness. Once again, alternatives 1, 2, and 3 outperform the baseline, but alternatives 2 and 3 offer significant improvements over both the baseline and alternative 1. Some degree of colocation of data types, whether it is accomplished physically or virtually, appears to significantly enhance performance in the case of multi-intelligence analysis.

Table 6.1 compares the overall performance of the baseline and alternatives.[2]

Figure 6.1
Commander's Awareness of Targets, One Intelligence Type (Abstracted)

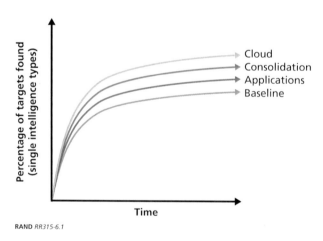

RAND RR315-6.1

---

[2]   Results for all of the metrics are detailed in Porche et al., 2013.

Figure 6.2
Commander's Awareness of Targets, Two or More Intelligence
Types (Abstracted)

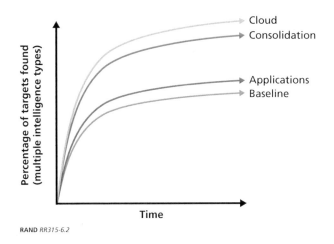

RAND *RR315-6.2*

Cost

The government's cost analysis of the baseline and alternatives concluded that the variance in lifecycle cost between each pair of options
was significant but not large.[3]

Risk

Our assessment of the risk associated with the baseline and each alternative reflects our estimate of the likelihood of an adverse event and the
severity of the consequences should that event occur. We considered
technical risk,[4] performance risk, and schedule risk in assessing each
option.

---

[3]   U.S. Department of the Navy, Center for Cost Analysis, "Distributed Common Ground
System–Navy (DCGS-N): Increment 2 AoA Cost Estimate Documentation," August 2012.
Note that the estimates used in the analysis were not intended to be "budget quality."

[4]   Technical risk itself has at least three components: design risk, threat risk, and require-
ments risk.

Table 6.1
Comparing the Performance of the Baseline and Alternatives

Alternative	Overall Performance	Explanation
Baseline	Poor across all measures	Performance is degraded by limited use of reachback, an information architecture that too frequently forwards raw data through the communications networks, and insufficient workflow automation.
Alternative 1: Applications	Better relative to the baseline	Performance relative to the baseline is improved through dynamic workload management and greater workflow automation.
Alternative 2: Consolidation	Good across all measures	Performance across all measures is good due to dynamic workload management and an efficient information architecture. The "brain" serves as an information clearinghouse that enables the consolidation of tools and data. This further enables workflow efficiencies and affords faster access to more data sources. Analyst ability to fuse multiple intelligence types improves.
Alternative 3: Cloud	Good across all measures; best across some measures	Performance across all measures is good, largely matching the performance levels of alternative 2. However, alternative 3 significantly reduces the strain on individual communications links because its effective metadata strategy reduces the need to share raw data feeds. This alternative's distributed cloud approach is far more scalable, compared to other options, in terms of data volume and sensor platforms that can be processed.

Risk analysis often involves some amount of subjectivity; for example, some may believe that cloud alternatives are inherently risky because of, for example, the complexities of making and keeping a cloud secure.[5] In this case, conducting an assessment of overall risk was challenging because the baseline and each of the alternatives scored very differently on individual measures of risk. For example, the baseline involves low technical risk because it does not require development

_____

[5] Security risks associated with cloud concepts in general are discussed in Neil Robinson, Lorenzo Valeri, Jonathan Cave, Tony G. Thompson-Starkey, Hans Graux, Sadie Creese, and Paul Hopkins, *The Cloud: Understanding the Security, Privacy and Trust Challenges*, Santa Monica, Calif.: RAND Corporation, TR-933-EC, 2011.

of new technologies and systems. On the other hand, the risk that it will not meet the Navy's performance needs is high. Conversely, alternative 3 (cloud) is likely to meet the Navy's performance needs, but, because it involves the most change (in terms of data strategy, database technology, organizational relationships, etc.), it involves greater technical risk.[6]

The baseline and each of the three alternatives involve risk, and there is no way to objectively rank their overall level of risk relative to one another without weighting individual risk categories. In our opinion, none of the four options is a clear "winner" in terms of being significantly less risky than the others.

---

[6] Porche et al. (2012) provide a detailed discussion of risk associated with specific cloud architectures.

CHAPTER SEVEN

Recommendations

If the Navy continues to field new and additional sensors as planned but does not change the way it collects, processes, exploits, and disseminates information, it will reach an ISR "tipping point"—the point at which intelligence analysts are no longer able to complete a minimum number of exploitation tasks within given time constraints—as soon as 2016.[1] As we have argued in previous chapters, a solution to the Navy's big data challenge must involve changes along four dimensions: people, tools and technology, data and data architectures, and demand and demand management. This means that the Navy needs

- more than just new tools; rather, it needs an approach to integrate them and make them more interoperable
- more than an adjustment in the number of analysts at each site; rather, it needs to manage analyst workload dynamically
- more than just an increase in the number of distinct intelligence sources that are available; rather, it needs a means to make them easy to find.[2]

---

[1] Brady et al., 2012; Porche et al., 2012; Porche et al., 2013. Today's budget environment will likely affect sensor procurement plans, so a delay in the tipping point is possible. Nonetheless, it looms.

[2] This report argues that no single program of record can completely solve the data flood problem. A materiel solution can improve today's existing capabilities, but, to meet the challenges of the future, the Navy needs new ways to manage people, manage demand, accommodate new tools and analytics, and, perhaps most importantly, manage data through efficient data strategies. Addressing just a single item on this list will be insufficient.

Move Forward with Alternative 3 (Cloud)

We recommend that the Navy move forward with alternative 3 (cloud). It offers significant potential performance improvements despite some technical and schedule risk. It is also (arguably) the alternative that is most amenable to future changes in information technology tools and applications.

Specifically, we recommend that the Navy adopt the IC's cloud approach, designing the next generation of Navy ISR tools and systems to work with the National Security Agency's distributed cloud concept (i.e., ICGovCloud). This information architecture should be sufficient to meet the growing volumes of data that will need to be harvested and thus enable viable TCPED operations in the future. Integrating and leveraging an IC-developed distributed cloud architecture will also better enable dynamic reachback for analysis and thus more-efficient use of manpower.

Alternative 3 represents a fundamental shift in how data are stored and shared within the DoD and IC. It relies on a data strategy that includes the use of metadata and the adoption of a common metadata catalogue, which is critical to achieving performance gains.[3]

Bandwidth limitations and other constraints on an information architecture are important design considerations. RAND modeling and simulation revealed that there are cloud designs—coupled with data strategies—that provide the best approach. We conclude that,

---

[3]   According to Programs, Management, Analytics & Technologies (2011),

> Metadata is the most effective way to minimize large data movement and to inform naval operators of the availability and content of shared data. . . . Although metadata is mandated in SECNAVINST 5000.36A, very little metadata is created across the . . . [Department of the Navy]. Part of the problem is legacy systems do not automatically tag their data as it is produced, and tagging the data manually is labor intensive. Tactical users are already time-constrained and often do not appreciate the larger enterprise usage of the data they manage.

The Defense Science Board Task Force on Integrating Sensor-Collected Intelligence specifically recommends that sensor-collected data be tagged with "meta-data as close to the sensor as possible using metadata that includes, at a minimum, time, location and sensor calibration" (Intelligence Science Board, 2008, p. 7).

with an efficient data strategy, the cloud option is the most scalable to increasing volumes of data from ISR sensors, even in a disconnected, interrupted, and low-bandwidth environment.

Extend Aspects and Components of Alternative 3 to Other Programs and Situations

Many aspects and components of alternative 3 can and should be extended to other programs and situations in the Navy:

- **Make a little command and control go a longer way.** When it comes to sharing the workload among analysts, flexible tasking and retasking, whether conducted regionally or globally, make significant productivity gains possible. Retaining relatively more personnel in reachback positions is desirable, but those gains are smaller when they are not coupled with dynamic management of analyst workload.
- **Integrate current technology.** Integration shortfalls hurt productivity. Because today's afloat and ashore analysts must work on multiple networks and with multiple software programs and databases, their workflow is often disjointed and their performance uneven. Improving integration may increase accuracy and timeliness in the development of situational awareness.
- **Make use of new information architectures.** New information architectures can help the right analyst find the right data at the right time and thus streamline analyst workflows. The Navy should work toward decreasing its dependence on stovepiped applications and segregated databases and networks.
- **Automate the workflow to the greatest extent possible.** Many of the rote tasks performed by afloat analysts could be automated through desktop software tools. Automating repetitive steps and keystrokes would free up time for the important business of acquiring data, exploiting them, and using the resulting knowledge to improve situational awareness. It would also improve the speed and efficiency of the process of fusing exploited products.

- **Tasking sensors smartly.** Inefficient transmission of useless data—such as hours of video of the open ocean—serves no purpose. Cueing sensors to a specific target would prevent the collection and transmission of unneeded raw data, thus lowering burdens on bandwidth and on analysts' cognitive reserves.

Prepare for Culture Change

Alternative 3 involves increased reliance on reachback personnel and reachback analytic capability. To reap the full benefits of the cloud solution, the Navy must embrace this dependency. However, some in the Navy's deployed community are predisposed to be skeptical of relying on analysis from the rear. Along with reasonable concerns, such as how this approach could falter in communications-denied environments, there is some measure of long-standing cultural bias against reliance on reachback capability. For example, the Navy's own historians recount that, as the use of wireless radios was becoming widespread in the early part of the 20th century, "there were captains and even admirals who were so reactionary in their views and so jealous of their prerogatives while on the high seas that they resented the idea of receiving orders by wireless. They opposed with might and main the new agency of communications."[4] In addition to tackling legitimate concerns associated with increased reliance on reachback, the Navy must be prepared to address the existing bias and ease the cultural shift that must accompany technological change. This will require significant effort.

---

[4] Gleason L. Archer, as quoted in Linwood S. Howeth, *History of Communications-Electronics in the United States Navy*, United States Government Printing Office: Washington, D.C., 1963, Chapter Six. It was the 1912 sinking of the *Titanic* that "highlighted the value of radio to ocean vessels" (Thomas H. White, "United States Early Radio History: Section Five," web page, undated).

Additional Information

Figure A.1
Comparing the Workload Tasking Options

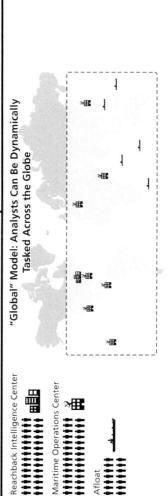

Current "Local" Model: Analysts Work
on Local Tasks Only

"Regional" Model: Analysts Can Be Dynamically
Tasked Within Their Region

"Global" Model: Analysts Can Be Dynamically
Tasked Across the Globe

Reachback Intelligence Center

Maritime Operations Center

Afloat

NOTE: Some locations are notional.

RAND RR315-A.1

Figure A.2
Further Illustration of the Options

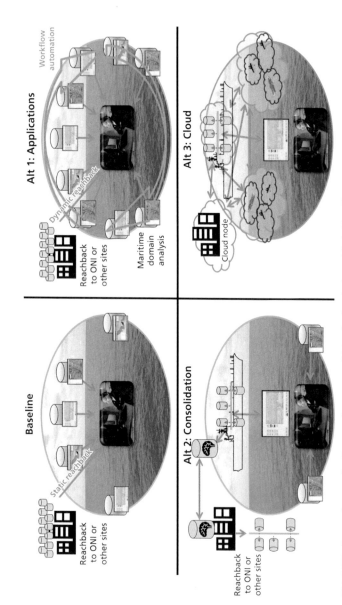

SOURCES: Screen images by Eugene Sergeev and Marcin Gardychowski via Fotolia.
NOTE: ONI = Office of Naval Intelligence.

RAND RR315-A.2

Table A.1
Additional Descriptions of the Baseline and Alternatives

Alternative	Design/Development Needed	Mean LISI Level	Sharing	Multi-Intelligence Fusing	Anticipated Effects	Resulting Environment
Baseline	No new design or development is conducted. Design and development are limited to planned sustainment and modernization activities.	Level 1: Connected (interoperability in a peer-to-peer environment)	There are separate databases, separate applications, separate services, and separate catalogs.	Fusion is accomplished "between the ears" of individual analysts.	No change.	Physical connectivity is established, allowing bits and bytes of data to be exchanged.
Alternative 1: Applications	Design and development are limited to integrating tools into the Navy's afloat (e.g., CANES) and ashore environments.	Level 2: Functional (interoperability in a distributed environment)	There are separate databases, separate applications, separate services, and separate catalogs.	Fusion is accomplished by individual analysts but enhanced by specific tools that "integrate" selected intelligence types.	Some workflow automation occurs locally across the workstation; capability gaps are addressed.	Heterogeneous systems exchanges are enabled, but separate data and applications remain prevalent. Some (minimal) common functions occur.

Table A.1—Continued

Alternative	Design/Development Needed	Mean LISI Level	Sharing	Multi-Intelligence Fusing	Anticipated Effects	Resulting Environment
Alternative 2: Consolidation	Design and development are required to make tools interoperable and to automate workflows afloat and ashore within the Navy's SOA environment.	Level 3: Domain (interoperability in an integrated Navy environment)	There are shared databases, separate applications, separate services, and shared catalogs (within the Navy).	Interoperability enables the integration of data of multiple intelligence types for tracked entities in a more-automatic fashion, allowing analysts to either quickly fuse multiple intelligence types or, in some cases, have it done automatically.	Services that enable the achievement of end-to-end workflow automation are made available by the hosting environment. The speed and accuracy of multi-intelligence fusion increase. Performance gaps are addressed. Sophisticated collaboration, simultaneous interactions, and event-triggered updates occur.	The global information environment is highly interoperable and distributed, "at one with the human operator."
Alternative 3: Cloud	Design and development are required to enable the Navy to ingest and process organic data for use with IC and DoD data in a cloud environment.	Level 4: Enterprise (interoperability in an IC/DoD environment)	There are shared databases, shared applications and widgets, shared services, and shared indices (across clouds).	Fusion of multiple intelligence types benefits from cloud-enabled reachback; efficiency and accuracy increase due to big data analytics; and ships can fuse locally collected data with data obtained from shore clouds through cloud-based technology.	The speed and accuracy of multi-intelligence fusion occurs through (1) greater utilization of organic data afloat and ashore; (2) more-seamless use of data across multiple security levels; and (3) the sharing of organic afloat sensor data to the wider Defense Intelligence Information Enterprise.	The cloud architecture is employed both afloat and ashore. So-called "mini-clouds" are employed afloat. The resulting data environment facilitates the use of big data analytics on data of all classifications.

Bibliography

9/11 Memorial, "USS Cole Bombing," web page, undated. As of December 23, 2013:
http://www.911memorial.org/uss-cole-bombing

Alkire, Brien, James G. Kallimani, Peter A. Wilson, and Louis R. Moore, *Applications for Navy Unmanned Aircraft Systems*, Santa Monica, Calif.: RAND Corporation, MG-957-NAVY, 2010. As of August 8, 2012:
http://www.rand.org/pubs/monographs/MG957.html

Bernard, Richard, *ELINT at NSA*, Center for Cryptologic History, National Security Agency, 2009. As of December 9, 2013:
http://www.nsa.gov/about/_files/cryptologic_heritage/publications/misc/elint.pdf

Brady, Ed, Jim Bexfield, Jim Hildegrand, and John Orem, "Analytical Approaches to Airborne ISR MORS Workshop: A Summary of Results from the Perspective of the Synthesis and Integration Group," presentation at the National Defense University, Washington, D.C., June 25, 2012. As of December 9, 2013:
http://www.mors.org/UserFiles/file/2012%20-%20Meeting%20UAS/MORS%20AISR%20outbrief.pdf

Brewin, Bob, "How a Misplaced Reef on a Digital Chart Destroyed a Navy Minesweeper," Nextgov.com, August 5, 2013. As of December 9, 2013:
http://www.nextgov.com/defense/2013/08/how-misplaced-reef-digital-chart-destroyed-navy-minesweeper/68126/

Burkhardt, Paul, and Chris Waring, "An NSA Big Graph Experiment," presentation at the Carnegie Mellon University SDI/ISTC Seminar, Pittsburgh, Pa., May 20, 2013. As of July 9, 2013:
http://www.pdl.cmu.edu/SDI/2013/slides/big_graph_nsa_rd_2013_56002v1.pdf

C4ISR Architectures Working Group, "Levels of Information Systems Interoperability (LISI)," 1998.

Card, Kendall, "Navy ISR Family of Systems: An Integrated Future," presentation at the Navy Information Dominance Industry Day, Chantilly, Va., March 7, 2012. As of December 9, 2013:
http://www.afcea.org/mission/intel/Presentation4.ppt

Chan, Y. K., and V. C. Koo, "An Introduction to Synthetic Aperture Radar (SAR)," *Progress in Electromagnetics Research B*, Vol. 2, 2008, pp. 27–60.

Christy, Julie, "Intel," *Garuda News*, Vol. 1, No. 3, April 2011. As of December 9, 2013: http://www.public.navy.mil/airfor/vaq134/Documents/VAQ-134%20 Garuda%20Newsletter/April%202011.pdf

Clark, Mike, "Fort Worth Firm AVX Aircraft Joins Bid for Navy Contract," *sUAS News*, December 1, 2011. As of December 9, 2013: http://www.suasnews.com/2011/12/10356/ fort-worth-firm-avx-aircraft-joins-bid-for-navy-contract/

Data Science Series, "Digital Universe Will Grow to 40ZB in 2020, with a 62% Share for Emerging Markets," blog post, December 13, 2012. As of December 11, 2013: http://datascienceseries.com/blog/ digital-universe-will-grow-to-40zb-in-2020-with-a-62-share-for-emerging-markets

Demchenko, Yuri, "Defining the Big Data Architecture Framework (BDAF)," presentation to the University of Amsterdam, July 14, 2013. As of January 6, 2014: http://bigdatawg.nist.gov/_uploadfiles/M0055_v1_7606723276.pdf

Deptula, David, "ISR Will Lead the Fight by 2020," *Breaking Defense,* June 24, 2011. As of December 9, 2013: http://breakingdefense.com/2011/06/isr-will-lead-the-fight-by-2020/

Dunn, Richard III, Price T. Bingham, and Charles A. "Bert" Fowler, "Ground Moving Target Indicator Radar and Transformation of U.S. Warfighting," Northrop Grumman, February 2004. As of August 31, 2012: http://www.northropgrumman.com/Capabilities/MPRTIP/Documents/gmti.pdf

Erwin, Marshall Curtis, *Intelligence, Surveillance, and Reconnaissance (ISR) Acquisition: Issues for Congress*, Congressional Research Service, R41284, December 27, 2011. As of December 9, 2013: http://www.fas.org/sgp/crs/intel/R41284.pdf

Fraden, Jacob, *Handbook of Modern Sensors: Physics, Designs, and Applications*, New York, N.Y.: Springer, 2010.

"Full Motion Progress," *Geospatial Intelligence Forum*, Vol. 8, No. 8, December 2010. As of December 9, 2013: http://www.kmimediagroup.com/old/mgt-home/292-gif-2010-volume-8-issue-8- december/3740-full-motion-progress.html

Gantz, John, Christopher Chute, Alex Manfrediz, Stephen Minton, David Reinsel, Wolfgang Schlichting, and Anna Toncheva, *The Diverse and Exploding Digital Universe: An Updated Forecast of Worldwide Information Growth Through 2011*, IDC Digital Universe Study, March 2008. As of July 18, 2013: http://www.emc.com/collateral/analyst-reports/diverse-exploding-digital-universe. pdf

Gantz, John, and David Reinsel, *As the Economy Contracts, the Digital Universe Expands*, IDC Digital Universe Study, May 2009. As of July 18, 2013:
http://www.emc.com/collateral/leadership/digital-universe/2009DU_final.pdf

———, *The Digital Universe Decade: Are You Ready?* IDC Digital Universe Study, May 2010. As of July 18, 2013:
http://www.emc.com/collateral/analyst-reports/idc-digital-universe-are-you-ready.pdf

———, *Extracting Value from Chaos*, IDC Digital Universe Study, June 2011. As of April 5, 2013:
http://www.itu.dk/people/rkva/2011-Fall-SMA/readings/ExtractingValuefromChaos.pdf

———, *The Digital Universe in 2020: Big Data, Bigger Digital Shadows, and Biggest Growth in the Far East*, IDC Digital Universe Study, December 2012. As of July 18, 2013:
http://idcdocserv.com/1414

Gantz, John, David Reinsel, Christopher Chute, Wolfgang Schlichting, John McArthur, Stephen Minton, Irida Xheneti, Anna Toncheva, and Alex Manfrediz, *The Expanding Digital Universe: A Forecast of Worldwide Information Growth Through 2010*, IDC Digital Universe Study, March 2007. As of July 18, 2013:
http://www.emc.com/collateral/analyst-reports/expanding-digital-idc-white-paper.pdf

Gertler, Jeremiah, *U.S. Unmanned Aerial Systems*, Congressional Research Service, R42136, January 3, 2012. As of December 9, 2013:
http://www.fas.org/sgp/crs/natsec/R42136.pdf

Hollis, Chuck, "Charting the Digital Universe: IDC's 6th Annual Study," blog post, December 11, 2012. As of December 11, 2013:
http://chucksblog.emc.com/chucks_blog/2012/12/charting-the-digital-universe-idcs-6th-annual-study.html

House Permanent Select Committee on Intelligence, *Performance Audit of Department of Defense Intelligence, Surveillance, and Reconnaissance*, April 2012. As of December 9, 2013:
http://intelligence.house.gov/sites/intelligence.house.gov/files/documents/ISRPerformanceAudit%20Final.pdf

Hovanessian, Shahen, *Introduction to Sensor Systems*, London and Boston, Mass.: Artech Publishers, 1988.

Howeth, Linwood S., *History of Communications-Electronics in the United States Navy*, United States Government Printing Office: Washington, D.C., 1963.

Hutchins, Susan G., Shelley P. Gallup, Doug MacKinnon, Gordon Schacher, and Scot Miller, "Enhancing Maritime Domain Awareness," presentation at the 13th International Command and Control Research and Technology Symposium, June 19, 2008.

IBM, "IBM Study: Digital Era Transforming CMO's Agenda, Revealing Gap in Readiness," IBM news release, October 11, 2011. As of December 9, 2013: http://www-03.ibm.com/press/us/en/pressrelease/35633.wss

Intelligence Science Board, *Integrating Sensor-Collected Intelligence*, Washington, D.C.: Office of the Under Secretary of Defense for Acquisition, Technology, and Logistics, November 2008. As of September 6, 2013: http://www.acq.osd.mil/dsb/reports/ADA491047.pdf

Joint Chiefs of Staff, *Department of Defense Dictionary of Military and Associated Terms*, November 8, 2010, as amended through July 15, 2012. As of August 31, 2012: http://www.dtic.mil/doctrine/new_pubs/jp1_02.pdf

Kar, Saroj, "Less Than 1% of the World's Information Is Being Analyzed: IDC Report," *Cloud Times*, December 27, 2012. As of April 5, 2013: http://cloudtimes.org/2012/12/27/world-information-analyzed-idc-report/

Kepner, Jeremy, Christian Anderson, William Arcand, David Bestor, Bill Bergeron, Chansup Byun, Matthew Hubbell, Peter Michaleas, Julie Mullen, David O'Gwynn, Andrew Prout, Albert Reuther, Antonio Rosa, and Charles Yee, "D4M 2.0 Schema: A General Purpose High Performance Schema for the Accumulo Database," paper presented at the 2013 IEEE High Performance Extreme Computing Conference, September 12, 2013.

Klimas, Jacqueline, "New System Expands Ships' Tracking Range," *Defense News*, July 24, 2012. As of August 31, 2012: http://www.defensenews.com/article/20120724/C4ISR01/307240012/ New-System-Expands-Ships-8217-Tracking-Range

L-3 ComCept, "NCCT: Network-Centric Collaborative Targeting Program," web page, undated. As of December 9, 2013: http://comceptinc.com/L3comcept/NCCT.htm

Lee, Caitlin, "AUVSI 2013: USMC's RQ-21A to Start Operational Testing in October," *IHS Jane's Defence Weekly*, August 13, 2013.

Lin, Jimmy, "MapReduce Is Good Enough? If All You Have Is a Hammer, Throw Away Everything That's Not a Nail!" *Big Data*, Vol. 1, No. 1, 2013, pp. 28–37.

Magnuson, Stew, "Military 'Swimming in Sensors and Drowning in Data,'" *National Defense Magazine*, January 2010. As of December 12, 2013: http://www.nationaldefensemagazine.org/archive/2010/January/Pages/Military%E 2%80%98SwimmingInSensorsandDrowninginData%E2%80%99.aspx

McKendrick, Joe, "Size of the Data Universe: 1.2 Zettabytes and Growing Fast," ZDNet.com, May 12, 2010a. As of April 5, 2013: http://www.zdnet.com/blog/service-oriented/ size-of-the-data-universe-1-2-zettabytes-and-growing-fast/4750

———, "Data Explosion: Enough to Fill DVDs Stretching to the Moon and Back," SmartPlanet.com, May 14, 2010b. As of July 18, 2013:
http://www.smartplanet.com/blog/business-brains/
data-explosion-enough-to-fill-dvds-stretching-to-the-moon-and-back/7010

Menthe, Lance, and Jeffrey Sullivan, *A RAND Analysis Tool for Intelligence, Surveillance, and Reconnaissance: The Collections Operations Model*, Santa Monica, Calif.: RAND Corporation, TR-557-AF, 2008. As of August 9, 2012:
http://www.rand.org/pubs/technical_reports/TR557.html

Miller, Greg, "MQ-4C BAMS UAS," presentation at the International Conference on Autonomous Unmanned Vehicles 2012, February 2012.

Miller, Rich, "'Digital Universe' to Add 1.8 Zettabytes in 2011," DataCenterKnowledge.com, June 28, 2011. As of April 5, 2013:
http://www.datacenterknowledge.com/archives/2011/06/28/
digital-universe-to-add-1-8-zettabytes-in-2011/

National Security Agency, "An Overview of Cloud Computing," *The Next Wave*, Vol. 14, No. 4, 2009, pp. 6–18. As of December 9, 2013:
http://www.nsa.gov/research/tnw/tnw174/articles/pdfs/TNW_17_4_Web.pdf

Naval Air Systems Command Public Affairs, "Navy Triton Unmanned Aircraft System Completes First Flight," story number NNS130522-20, 2013. As of December 23, 2013:
http://www.navy.mil/submit/display.asp?story_id=74320

"Navy Extends X-47B Unmanned Aircraft System Test Program at Pax," InsideDefense.com, August 9, 2013.

Office of Naval Intelligence, "Nimitz Operational Intelligence Center," web page, last updated September 24, 2013. As of December 9, 2013:
http://www.oni.navy.mil/commands/Nimitz.html

Office of Naval Research, "Big Data Tutorial," v1.00, slide deck, February 21, 2012.

Office of the Chief of Naval Operations, "Distributed Common Ground System–Navy (DCGS-N) Increment 2 Analysis of Alternatives (AoA) Study Plan/Scope & Tasking Directive," version 2-8, 2011.

Oracle.com, "Oracle® Database SecureFiles and Large Objects Developer's Guide, 11g Release 1 (11.1)," web page, undated. As of December 12, 2013:
http://docs.oracle.com/cd/B28359_01/appdev.111/b28393/adlob_intro.
htm#ADLOB001

Osborn, Kris, "Navy Delays Triton UAS Development," *DefenseTech*, April 11, 2013. As of August 21, 2013:
http://defensetech.org/2013/04/11/navy-delays-triton-uas-development

Pavlo, Andrew, Erik Paulson, Alexander Rasin, Daniel J. Abadi, David J. DeWitt, Samuel Madden, and Michael Stonebraker, "A Comparison of Approaches to Large-Scale Data Analysis," *SIGMOD '09: Proceedings of the 35th SIGMOD International Conference on Management of Data*, 2009, pp. 165–178.

Pieper, Steve, "Maritime ISR Enterprise," presentation at the Office of Naval Intelligence, July 2011.

Porche, Isaac R. III, James Dryden, Kathryn Connor, Bradley Wilson, Shawn McKay, Kate Giglio, and Juan Montelibano, *Finding Services for an Open Architecture: A Review of Existing Applications and Programs in PEO C4I*, Santa Monica, Calif.: RAND Corporation, MG-1071-NAVY, 2011. As of January 3, 2014:
http://www.rand.org/pubs/monographs/MG1071

Porche, Isaac R. III, Evan Saltzman, Roland Yardley, and Gordon Lee, "MAXINT," presentation at the Military Operations Research Workshop on Analytic Approaches to Airborne ISR, National Defense University, Ft. McNair, Washington, D.C., April 2012. Not available to the general public.

Porche, Isaac R. III, Bradley Wilson, Shane Tierney, Ray Koym, James Dryden, Evan Saltzman, Roland J. Yardley, John M. Yurchak, Stephanie Young, Endy M. Daehner, Megan McKernan, and Kate Giglio, *The DCGS-Navy Increment 2 Analysis of Alternatives: Options for Meeting the TCPED Challenges and Opportunities*, Santa Monica, Calif.: RAND Corporation, 2013. Not available to the general public.

Program Executive Office, Command, Control, Communications, Computers, and Intelligence, "PEO C4I Masterplan," version 5.0, August 7, 2011a.

———, "PEO C4I Tactical Cloud," October 2011b.

Programs, Management, Analytics & Technologies, "Maritime ISR Enterprise Acquisition (MIEA) Review," white paper, January 2011. As of December 5, 2012:
http://www.pmatllc.com/whitepapers/MIEA_WhitePaper_FINAL_Signed.pdf

Rafique, Ansar, "Evaluating NOSQL Technologies for Historical Financial Data," Department of Information Technology, Uppsala University, January 2013.

Riccitelli, Robert, "John C. Stennis Carrier Strike Group N6 Post Deployment Brief: 27 July 2011–02 March 2012," presentation at the 33rd annual U.S. Navy–U.S. Marine Corps Spectrum Management Conference, San Diego, Calif., March 2012. As of December 11, 2013:
http://www.dtic.mil/get-tr-doc/pdf?AD=ADA559652

Riposo, Jessie, John Gordon IV, Robert Murphy, Bradley Wilson, and Isaac R. Porche III, *CANES Contracting Strategies for Full Deployment*, Santa Monica, Calif.: RAND Corporation, TR-993-NAVY, 2012. As of January 6, 2014:
http://www.rand.org/pubs/technical_reports/TR993

Robinson, Neil, Lorenzo Valeri, Jonathan Cave, Tony G. Thompson-Starkey, Hans Graux, Sadie Creese, and Paul Hopkins, *The Cloud: Understanding the Security, Privacy and Trust Challenges*, Santa Monica, Calif.: RAND Corporation, TR-933-EC, 2011. As of November 3, 2013: http://www.rand.org/pubs/technical_reports/TR933.html

Rosenberg, Barry, "Battlefield Network Connects Allied Forces in Afghanistan," DefenseSystems.com, September 14, 2010. As of December 23, 2013: http://defensesystems.com/articles/2010/09/02/c4isr-2-afghan-mission-network-connects-allies.aspx

"RQ-4 Global Hawk Uavs Prepare for Maritime Role," *Defense Industry Daily*, September 10, 2013. As of December 9, 2013: http://www.defenseindustrydaily.com/global-hawk-uav-prepares-for-maritime-role-updated-01218/

Schnurr, Mary Lynn, "Distributed Analysis, Processing Capabilities Empower Warfighters," *Signal Online*, January 2008. As of December 11, 2013: http://www.afcea.org/signal/articles/templates/SIGNAL_Article_Template.asp?articleid=1455&zoneid=3

Scutro, Andrew, "Admiral: Complacency Caused Sub Collision," *Navy Times*, October 29, 2009. As of July 17, 2013: http://www.navytimes.com/news/2009/10/navy_hartford_lessons_102809w/

Serena, Chad C., Isaac R. Porche III, Joel B. Predd, Jan Osburg, and Bradley Lossing, *Lessons Learned from the Afghan Mission Network: Developing a Coalition Contingency Network*, Santa Monica, Calif.: RAND Corporation, forthcoming.

Shaffer, Greg, "It's All About the Data," presentation to the Armed Forces Communications and Electronics Association, August 21, 2012.

Summe, Jack, "Navy's New Strategy and Organization for Information Dominance," *CHIPS: The Department of the Navy's Information Technology Magazine*, January–March 2010. As of August 29, 2012: http://www.doncio.navy.mil/CHIPS/ArticleDetails.aspx?ID=2557

Taylor, Dan, "As Fire Scout Deployments Grow, Navy Seeks Beefed-Up Version," *Defense News*, August 28, 2012.

Thusoo, Ashish, Joydeep Sen Sarma, Namit Jain, Zheng Shao, Prasad Chakka, Suresh Anthony, Hao Liu, Pete Wyckoff, and Raghotham Murthy, "Hive: A Warehousing Solution Over a Map-Reduce Framework," Very Large Data Base Endowment Inc., 2009. As of December 11, 2013: http://www.vldb.org/pvldb/2/vldb09-938.pdf

U.S. Department of Defense, *Quadrennial Defense Review Report*, Washington, D.C., February 6, 2006. As of September 23, 2013: http://www.defense.gov/qdr/report/report20060203.pdf

———, *Quadrennial Defense Review Report,* Washington, D.C., February 2010. As of September 23, 2013:
http://www.defense.gov/qdr/images/QDR_as_of_12Feb10_1000.pdf

U.S. Department of the Navy, *Distributed Common Ground System–Navy (DCGS-N) Technical Manual,* EE685-1N-SAM-010, 2009a.

———, "E-2 HAWKEYE Early Warning and Control Aircraft," United States Navy fact file, last updated February 5, 2009b. As of December 11, 2013:
http://www.navy.mil/navydata/fact_display.asp?cid=1100&tid=700&ct=1

———, "P-3C *ORION* Long Range ASW Aircraft," United States Navy fact file, last updated February 18, 2009c. As of December 11, 2013:
http://www.navy.mil/navydata/fact_display.asp?cid=1100&tid=1400&ct=1

———, "FID/FIAF Frequently Asked Questions," current as of January 2010a. As of December 11, 2013:
http://www.public.navy.mil/bupers-npc/officer/Detailing/IDC_FAO/intelligence/Documents/FIDFIAF.pdf

———, *Navy Training System Plan for the Maritime Domain Awareness (MDA) Spiral 1,* Washington, D.C., N6-NTSP-E-70-0801, June 22, 2010b.

———, "Medium Range Maritime Unmanned Aerial System (MRMUAS) Broad Agency Announcement (BAA)," solicitation number N00019-11-R-0089, last updated on February 27, 2012. As of December 11, 2013:
https://www.fbo.gov/index?s=opportunity&mode=form&id=23ccfa9ca1902f00f79fa15edc0a90bd&tab=core&_cview=1

U.S. Department of the Navy, Center for Cost Analysis, "Distributed Common Ground System–Navy (DCGS-N): Increment 2 AoA Cost Estimate Documentation," August 2012. Not available to the general public.

U.S. Navy Naval Air Systems Command, "Navy Awards $1.9B for Fourth Phase of P-8A Production, Readies for First Deployment," NAVAIR news release, August 1, 2013. As of August 21, 2013:
http://www.navair.navy.mil/index.cfm?fuseaction=home.PrintNewsStory&id=5429

"U.S. Navy Vessels in Bahrain for Evaluation After Collision," CNN.com, March 21, 2009. As of January 6, 2014:
http://edition.cnn.com/2009/WORLD/meast/03/21/navy.vessels.collide/index.html?iref=mpstoryview

U.S. Pacific Fleet Public Affairs, "USS Guardian Grounding Investigation Results Released," June 20, 2013. As of December 11, 2013:
http://www.navy.mil/submit/display.asp?story_id=74930

U.S. Secretary of Defense, "Action Agenda to Support 'End Strength' Memo Tasks," memorandum, August 25, 2003. As of January 3, 2014:
http://library.rumsfeld.com/doclib/sp/3004/2003-08-25%20to%20the%20
Secretaries%20of%20the%20Military%20Departments%20re%20Action%20
Agenda%20to%20Support%20End%20Strength%20Memo%20Tasks.pdf

Venner, Jason, *Pro Hadoop: Build Scalable, Distributed Applications in the Cloud,* Berkeley, Calif.: A Press, 2009.

Vijayan, Jaikumar, "Facebook Moves 30-Petabyte Hadoop Cluster to New Data Center," *ComputerWorld*, July 29, 2011. As of December 11, 2013:
http://www.computerworld.com/s/article/9218752/
Facebook_moves_30_petabyte_Hadoop_cluster_to_new_data_center

White, Thomas H., "United States Early Radio History: Section Five," web page, undated. As of January 10, 2014:
http://earlyradiohistory.us/sec005.htm

"Winter: Navy Will Re-Examine Unmanned Assets as They Reach Fleet," InsideDefense.com, August 10, 2012.

Wu, Haiqing, D. Grenier, G. Y. Delisle, and Da-Gang Fang, "Translational Motion Compensation in ISAR Image Processing," *IEEE Transactions on Image Processing*, Vol. 4, No. 11, November 1995, pp. 1561–1570.